FOUL DEEDS AND SUSPICIOUS DEATHS IN NOTTINGHAM

'FOUL DEEDS AND SUSPICIOUS DEATHS' Series

Foul Deeds and Suspicious Deaths series explores in detail crimes of passion, brutal murders, grisly deeds and foul misdemeanours. From Victorian street crime, to more modern murder where passion, jealousy, or social depravation brought unexpected violence to those involved. From mysterious death to murder and manslaughter, the books are a fascinating insight into not only those whose lives are forever captured by the suffering they endured, but also into the society that moulded and shaped their lives. Each book takes you on a journey into the darker and unknown side of the area.

Other titles in the series

Other Local Books of Interest

Please contact us via any of the methods below for more information or a catalogue.

WHARNCLIFFE BOOKS

47 Church Street • Barnsley • South Yorkshire • S70 2AS

Tel: 01226 734555 • 734222   Fax: 01226 734438

E-mail: enquiries@pen-and-sword.co.uk • **Website:** www.wharncliffebooks.co.uk

Foul Deeds and Suspicious Deaths In
NOTTINGHAM

KEVIN TURTON

Series Editor
Brian Elliott

Wharncliffe Books

First Published in 2003 by
Wharncliffe Books
an imprint of
Pen and Sword Books Limited,
47 Church Street, Barnsley,
South Yorkshire. S70 2AS

Copyright © Kevin Turton 2003

*For up-to-date information on other titles produced under the
Wharncliffe imprint, please telephone or write to:*

**Wharncliffe Books
FREEPOST
47 Church Street
Barnsley
South Yorkshire S70 2BR
Telephone (24 hours): 01226 734555**

ISBN: 1-903425-35-2

A CIP catalogue record of this book is available from the
British Library

Cover illustration: *Front – Tragedy at Nottingham.* Courtesy of Steve Jones
Rear – The dying deposition. Courtesy of Steve Jones

Printed in the United Kingdom by
CPI UK

Contents

Introduction

True crime rarely mirrors fiction in terms of plot and readers of it do not have to be adept at understanding the idiosyncratic personalities of its investigating officers. What they do have to possess however, is curiosity, compassion and a need to better understand those whose lives were either broken or irrevocably changed by the events they suffered or witnessed. It is a fact that in most cases of murder both killer and victim are known to each other, and by the time of any inquest we, the public at large, have come to know them also. It is as unavoidable as it is necessary. The public arena in which any subsequent investigation is carried out and the avid newspaper reportage that follows ensures our involvement is inevitable. We follow each story as it unfolds, discuss its merits, or otherwise, across the breakfast table and search out further information through television news channels or the Internet. Things have not changed in any fundamental way over the years. Those who peopled our towns and cities a hundred years ago were no different to us in the way they viewed murder, suicide or suspicious death. They too sought out the facts, felt for the victims, suffered for the families and in the main, were at one with the verdicts handed down by the courts. But for them it was possibly more personal. Inquests were generally held in the nearest public room to the crime scene, often a public house, where the jurors were free to view the body and if known, name the perpetrator of the crime. In Nottingham, Quarter Sessions were held in the city, (as were executions) and detailed reportage through various regional newspapers, ensured most facts were printed verbatim. In fact it is these very same newspapers that are key to modern research. Their meticulous coverage of events relevant to the city has ensured a permanent record has been maintained for historians to access and I thank them for it. Along with various records and writers in other genres, they have provided source material for the book you now read.

Foul Deeds and Suspicious Deaths in Nottingham is a collection of events that captured the attention of previous generations. These events could be described as macabre, mysterious, suspicious and dark, for they always resulted in death. Equally they once held the attention of a city whose inquisitive populace, not unlike today, had a thirst for the tenebrous side of human nature.

For those involved it must have been a desperate time. In retelling the circumstance and consequence of each incident it is important to remember that these are true events and the people involved had real lives. There is no artistic licence here. From the desperation of Thomas Greensmith who murdered all his children, to the suspicious death of Florence Weatherall beside the Nottingham to Mansfield road, these are stories of people whose lives once held the attention of those who lived and worked in the city. Through their stories we glimpse the past and possibly better understand, not only the public perception of justice prevalent at the time, but also the living conditions that often led to these sort of crimes in the first place.

This has been a journey along which I have met many people. Amongst those I have come to know there are those I would have no wish to ever have met in life. Thomas Gray, James Turner and Samuel Atherley to name but three are deserving of their place in the lists of the infamous. Yet there are others for whom I can only feel sympathy. Whether or not you share my view is immaterial – what is important is that you too enjoy the journey.

Finally, there are those I must thank for their unstinting support throughout the research for this book. The staff of the local studies section of Nottingham library who assisted greatly in the sourcing of material, in particular photographs of areas in and around the city that are contemporary with the period covered. The various unknown newspaper reporters who gave such in depth and vivid accounts of crime over the years to their readers and Maureen Yule, whose unquestioning help ensured this book reached its final conclusion. Over the last year she has travelled miles in pursuit of photographic locations I could use and her map reading skills have probably been greatly enhanced as a result. My thanks to all.

Chapter 1

Pity the Poor Children –
The Basford Murders
1837

Thomas Greensmith had endured a difficult year. Since the death of his wife in March 1836 he had struggled to hold down a job whilst trying to handle the day-to-day needs of his four children. Ranging from the ages of two to nine years, they dominated his days and made stable work difficult to find and harder to hold onto. By January of 1837 he had moved the family to a cottage in Basford and taken a job as a bleacher for which he received thirteen shillings (65p) a week, his son John being the eldest at nine years old, he placed in a rope yard for which he received a further one shilling and sixpence (7.5p). Things were looking up and when his father-in-law agreed that if he could have his meals cooked at the cottage each day he would pay a weekly board of six shillings (30p), Thomas was able to hire a housekeeper, which he did in late February.

Ann Fryer was a widow, engaged initially by Thomas on a month by month basis, she was to have a room in the cottage, would be responsible for general cleaning, looking after the children and cooking all the food. It was an arrangement that suited her well. She needed a roof over her head, had run a house before, albeit small scale, and knew enough to cook simple meals. Throughout March the arrangement seemed to work quite well but by April, for some reason she was never to know, Thomas had obviously cooled on the idea and found someone to replace her. He told her at the start of the month that it would be her last and she was to find another position by May. Ann Fryer, unperturbed by the prospect of impending unemployment, took the news philosophically. It had happened to her before and probably would again. Finding another post she obviously did not feel would be too difficult a task.

Ordnance Survey Map of Old Basford, c.1890. Nottingham City Library

On the night of 3 April, two days after this conversation, Thomas returned from work at his usual time of 7 pm. After eating supper he sat talking to Benjamin Oxspring, his father-in-law until around eight o'clock then, as had become his custom, he left to go drinking. At some time after eleven that same night Joseph Woodward, father of Thomas's landlord roused Ann Fryer from her bed demanding rent. This was the first she knew of any outstanding arrears on the place or any kind of financial difficulties and expressed her obvious surprise, but Woodward was not a man to discuss his business with a housekeeper. Disappointed he had not been able to find Thomas home, and unwilling to wait, he made to leave. At that moment, fortuitously or otherwise, depending on your point of view, Thomas Greensmith walked in through the cottage door. He, like Woodward, had no desire to stand in front of Ann Fryer, airing his dirty linen in public, so held the door wide for them both to step out into the yard where no one could over hear their conversation.

Joseph Woodward walked as far as the passage entrance and told Thomas in no uncertain terms that he wanted the rent paid at nine o'clock the next morning. Thomas remonstrated vehemently, insisting he had made an arrangement with Joseph's son, Mark, who he considered to be his landlord, that the rent was to be paid on the following Wednesday, a week away. There followed a heated exchange and Joseph, not prepared to wait a further week, regardless of any arrangement that may or may not have been made with his son, was adamant that if the rent did not appear in the morning then he would seize all the goods in the house and evict the family.

It was a short argument, no more than a few minutes, but its impact upon Thomas was profound in the extreme. Returning to the cottage he told Ann Fryer to pack a bag and leave. Angered at such a suggestion, she argued fiercely against his right to act so unfairly and at such a time of night. But Thomas Greensmith was immoveable, nothing Ann Fryer could say or do was going to dissuade him, she had to go. He waited impatiently as she dressed then locked the door after her as she left.

In a state of high anxiety he sat by the fire in the kitchen and waited in the darkness for over an hour. At some time around 1 am, believing his children to be asleep, he lit a candle then walked slowly upstairs and into the bedroom at the front of the house. Inside, the children slept two to a bed, the youngest in the bed nearest the door, the other two under the window. Pausing briefly to check they were all sound asleep, he took a handkerchief from his pocket and walked over to the bed containing the two youngest children. Placing the candle on the floor he sat beside them, kissed each child in turn, careful to shake them by the hand as he did so, then wrapped the handkerchief around each of their necks and strangled them.

Shocked at what he had done he reclaimed the candle, stood up from the bed and returned downstairs. It took him about half an hour sat in front of a cold fire grate to realise in his own words: 'I might as well suffer for them all, as for them two.'

So taking up the candle again he returned to the bedroom. John, the eldest boy, was sound asleep, William who shared his bed, was not. Seeing the candle reappear in the doorway he leapt from the bed and ran across the room to the other bed where he pushed in beside his dead brother and sister. Thomas ignored him and in an almost mechanical fashion placed the handkerchief around the sleeping boys neck and sat beside him until satisfied he was dead. At this point William sat up and fearing for his life called out. But Thomas was resolute and within minutes the last of his four children lay dead. Returning to the kitchen he sat in the dark for an hour then, concerned he would never see his children again, he went back into the bedroom. Going to each child in turn he shook their hand then sat beside the three that lay dead together until dawn.

At a quarter to seven in the morning Charlotte Watson, who lived next door to the Greensmith family, was awoken by the sound of someone knocking at her neighbour's door. Aware of the time and familiar with the Greensmiths usual habits she went downstairs with the intention of rousing Ann Fryer. The young boy she had seen doing the knocking she knew, he came around to the house most mornings to wake John and go with him to the rope yard. She also knew that if he had to knock then something was most definitely amiss. After a few fruitless minutes stood outside the house trying to get some sort of response from Ann she sent the boy off to work and pushed open the front door. Stepping inside, she noted the house was unusually quiet, no fires had been laid, no food had been cooked, the children were not charging around as they ought to have been at that time of the morning, and even more sinister, there was no sign of Ann Fryer. Stealing herself she made her way gingerly upstairs and eased open the door to the bedroom in which she knew the children always slept. In the half light it appeared at first as if they were still sleeping, Thomas had covered them in blankets before leaving earlier that morning as if trying to keep them warm, but as she uncovered each in turn the truth of what had taken place in that house during the night became all too clear.

In an understandable panic she fled the scene and ran to another neighbour, Mrs Birkett. Here she found Ann Fryer still in bed and after blurting out all that she had seen the three of them returned to the Greensmith house. After a cursory examination of the four bodies they sent out for Dr William Morley, local surgeon, who made a more thorough examination and

Old Town Gaol, St John Street, c.1890. Nottingham City Library

confirmed all four children had been strangled.

Whilst all this was taking place Thomas Greensmith was five miles away in the *Robin Hood* public house at Lambley. After leaving Basford around dawn he had first walked into Nottingham then on to Carlton and finally on to Lambley because he knew John Brownlow, landlord of the pub and a long time friend. He was still in the bar at nine o'clock that same night when Brownlow's sister walked in and started telling everyone about the child murders in Basford. As she regaled all around with the gory story she had heard and gave out a description of the man police believed to have committed the killings, Brownlow recognised in her narrative the face of his friend. Quietly and without alerting anyone else in the bar he had someone sent out to fetch Collishaw, the local policeman. It took about an hour for him to arrive by which time talk around the bar had drifted onto other subjects and Greensmith had retired to the corner of the room to sit alone beside the fire. The policeman made no immediate arrest, choosing instead to order a jug of beer and join him at his table where the two men talked for some time. It was during this conversation that Collishaw realised John Brownlow's suspicions had been well founded and once Greensmith had confirmed his address in Basford there was no going back.

Thomas Greensmith's next public appearance was two days later. On the morning of 5 April Mr C Swann, coroner, held an inquest inside the *Fox and Crown Inn* at Basford and he was brought from Nottingham prison to attend. Crowds outside the inn had been growing all morning and by the time of his arrival the throng had spilled out into the street, all desperate to catch a glimpse of the multiple murderer. Greensmith himself remained calm throughout, apparently unperturbed by the jostling crowd which met his hackney carriage or the proceedings that were about to damn him. After being hustled inside he maintained this dispassionate exterior, listening to the opening charges calmly and showing little sign of remorse as he waited for the jury to file past the four bodies that lay in an adjacent room. When asked to give the court the names and ages of the children he had murdered he did so with great composure.

Most of the morning was taken up by testimony from the women who had found or seen the bodies on the morning of the killings. As the hearing drifted into the afternoon it was left to Thomas Greensmith to either deny his guilt or offer up mitigating circumstances for the murders. He spoke clearly, explaining his usual routine to the court and his meeting with Joseph Woodward about the rent arrears in the back yard of his cottage that so upset him:

...I told him I had agreed with his son to pay it next Wednesday but one; he told me he would have it next morning; I told him that was impossible, but I would pay him in a week, he said he would not be put off o'that'n he would have it in the morning, or he would take my goods. I thought if he took my goods, I should have no-where to go - nor no home, nor nothing and I that before my children should be turned into the street in that way, I'd suffer what the law should please to clap on me...

The coroner cautioned Greensmith as to the evidence he had decided to give the court, concerned that he was about to condemn himself. He was right. Thomas Greensmith had no intentions of trying to mitigate his actions. He saw them as necessary, something a caring father would do for his children,

I was not willing to part with my children and I strangled them with my handkerchief.

There was nothing else to add. There was almost no consultation amongst the jurors, their verdict of wilful murder was inevitable and took only a few minutes to deliver. Naming, as they could in 1837, Thomas Greensmith as the murderer.

The journey back to Nottingham was difficult. The crowds that had continued to gather outside the *Fox and Crown Inn* throughout the hearing had become more vociferous in their condemnation. They surrounded the Hackney as it left Basford and followed in its wake as it made its way to Nottingham's prison hurling abuse throughout the short journey.

At nine o'clock on 28 July the Honourable Sir James Allan Park presided over Nottingham's summer assizes. Thomas Greensmith, after spending three months in prison, was brought before the court and formally charged with murdering his four

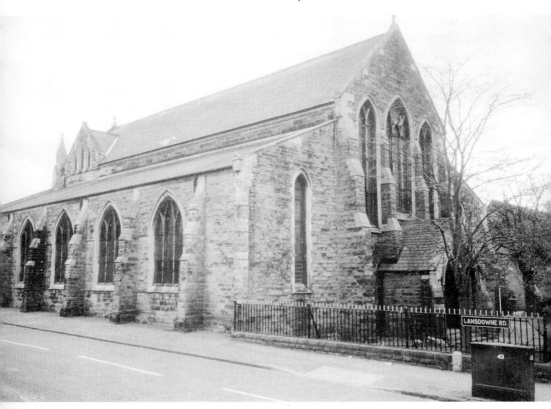

Old Basford Church. The author

children, nine year old John, seven year old William, five year old Ann and two year old Mark. The prosecution, led by Mr Wildman, opened the case by instructing the jury that they could only accept insanity as a cause of the murder if they could form the opinion that,

> *...the unhappy man was not at the time in a situation to distinguish right from wrong...*

Thomas Greensmith had no legal representation and was, therefore, dependent upon the judge to ensure this possibility was explored. It was to be a difficult day, though, as he had shown at the inquest, Greensmith was not overawed by the mechanics of the court, nor was he to show signs of contrition.

As he took the stand after listening to the morning's evidence from those who had attended the Inquest he reiterated his statement of twelve weeks earlier. There was only one key difference to what he had told the coroners' court. Having had time to reflect upon this earlier statement he added the stimulus or inducement for murder had come from his discussion with Joseph Woodward, 'The threat that Mr Woodward gave me caused me to do what I did.'

It was a clear attempt to say to the court that he was not in control of his actions when he murdered the four children. The judge had Henry Attenburrow brought to the stand. As surgeon to the county gaol he was considered medically competent to decide upon Greensmith's state of mind throughout his brief incarceration though not to express that as an opinion. He was expected only to give, if you like, an overview of how his prisoners behaviour could have been as a result of some external influence. Whether or not some event could have triggered his actions. Attenburrow had no doubt as to Thomas Greensmith's mental state and no hesitation in stating the facts to the court. According to the evidence he gave it had been clear from the first day the two men met that something was seriously amiss:

> *...the pupils of his eyes were much dilated and there was great anxiety and wildness about their expression, and that irritation had continued since. The tongue too was far from healthy, but in that peculiar state which indicates insanity... judging from all the circumstances of the case, was decidedly of the opinion that the man was insane at the time of the perpetration of the act.*

But the judge demurred to accept any opinion as to the state of mind of Greensmith. He was of the view that an opinion of this type, founded on facts sequent to the act that had brought him to trial was unacceptable. There followed some legal debate at the end of which the judge was handed a legal reference, which after considering in detail caused him to modify his objections. Henry Attenburrow was then allowed to expand upon the sentiment he had expressed. Though at its conclusion Judge Sir James Allan Park still refused to recognise the opinion he had given and told the court in no uncertain terms:

> *His mode of forming opinions would tend to acquit all the*

prisoners. No conviction could be obtained, if such opinions were to be relied on.

There were no dissenting voices.

As if to reinforce the judge's view that insanity was not an argument he viewed with any validity, Samuel Wilkinson, a police constable, was called to give evidence. He testified that shortly after Greensmith's arrest a pair of children's boots had been found and proven to have belonged to his son, John. Greensmith, having been shown these boots, confirmed he had taken them from his son immediately after the murders and sold them the same morning, therefore strengthening the courts view that if the prisoner before the Bar had been uncertain of his acts before killing his children, he had certainly been aware of them afterwards; a point not lost on the jury who took only twelve minutes to return a guilty verdict. There was no dissent from the bench nor any from Thomas Greensmith who had sat throughout resigned to the inevitability of the day. As the sentence of death was passed he remained, as he had been since his arrest, passionless and calm.

Chapter 2

A Walk in the Wood –
The Colwick Killings
1844

It could be said of William Saville that he was a man of poor intellect, having never attended a school at any stage of his life, which meant he could neither read nor write. Though he had borne the handicap well throughout his twenty-nine or thirty years. So there was little reason that he would ever have agreed with any such notion. What would be a fairer assessment of his character would be that he had never really been able to climb out of the poverty this lack of education had ensured he must endure, whilst uncertainty about his age, which came from his father's inability to recall the year of his birth, had probably always caused him a niggling doubt as to his paternal origins. Perhaps if his mother had lived beyond his infancy, life would have dealt the cards a little more evenly.

For seven years he had worked as a farm labourer in Blidworth, Bestwood Park and Gedling, returning to Arnold, the place in which he was born, just after his nineteenth birthday. At this stage of his life, after years spent toiling in the fields, where the weather at best could be uncertain, he had decided that he wanted to leave the land and work at something that would not leave him at the mercy of the seasons. In due course his father found him a position in Daybrook, as a framework knitter. Here, he moved in 1833 to work and lodge with George Lynch who had offered to train him in the necessary skills. For the next three years he learned his craft and found, perhaps surprisingly, it was a skill that came to him very readily.

In the spring of 1836, having settled into his new life, he met a woman, some eight years older than himself. Originally from Spalding in Lincolnshire, she had been working in service to a Captain Kelsey who lived on Long Row in Nottingham. At the

Long Row West, Nottingham, c.1845. Nottingham City Library

start of that year she had been seriously ill and after a partially successful operation to remove a cyst from her eye had rendered the eye blind, she had been sent to Daybrook to convalesce. Ann Ward was thirty years old. To William, who cared little for age, she was a very happy distraction from the life he had chosen to lead, though it is doubtful he ever considered their relationship would develop into anything more meaningful. Ann's sister, Harriet Brownsword, and a woman known only as Mrs Hart had other ideas. By the summer of 1836 it was clear Ann was pregnant. According to the two women who turned up unexpectedly on his doorstep she was five months pregnant and the child was to be his. Unconvinced, for whatever reason, and not about to allow his single status to be irrevocably changed, he refused to marry her. They in turn threatened him with violence, which had little effect, then, not to be outdone, resorted to a little subterfuge. Plying him with gin one Saturday in July they

Long Row West, Nottingham today. Nottingham City Library

took him into Nottingham on a pretext. Ann's sister was at that time in service to a gentleman who lived in the middle of the city and William, by far the worse for wear through drink, was taken to this house and kept in the kitchen. On the Sunday the two women filled him full of gin and on Monday he was dragged to a church and married.

The marriage was destined from that point on to be unsuccessful and so it proved. Immediately after the ceremony William returned to his father's house at Arnold whilst Ann went to live in Stanhope Street. Shortly after the birth they moved together into a house in Red Street at Meadow Platts where they stayed for just over a year. Unfortunately, the new baby died within four months and Ann began work binding shoes and boots for 1s 6d (7.5p) a week. The marriage by now was in decline, Ann was obviously dissatisfied with the way the relationship was developing and she left toward the end of 1836. Before meeting with William she had lived with a Mr Buchan on High Pavement; this was where she returned, staying for about ten months before being reconciled with her husband.

The next seven years were reasonably stable. Their daughter, Mary, was born in 1837, Harriet in 1839 and as 1840 dawned she was pregnant with their third child, Thomas. But cracks had begun to reappear in the marriage and by early spring of the same year William had deserted her, forcing her into the workhouse. He, in turn, was arrested and imprisoned, serving three months hard labour. On being released he quickly discovered Ann had given birth to his son and also moved back into the city. After a short search amongst people they both knew he tracked her down and moved back with her. They would live at three different addresses over the next three years.

By Christmas 1843, though things were so bad between the two, they decided on a final split. William was out of work, they were both suffering from the 'itch' (scabies) and the house was lice-bound. There was no alternative to finding somewhere else to live. Realising that, William seized the opportunity of making it a permanent break, but having already served one prison sentence for desertion he wanted the split to be amicable and secret. Both agreed to tell any that asked that Ann had gone to live with her brother in Lincolnshire. William knew she had kept up the contact and wrote frequent letters to the farm at Long Sutton. It would, he probably argued, be a logical place for her to go, for whatever reason she agreed. By New Year's Day 1844 William was living and working in Radford. Ann, who had not moved to Lincolnshire, was back in the workhouse.

Over the years William had developed a friendship with a family named Sutton. Living in Radford, employing men skilled as frame work-knitters and able to take in a lodger, it was an obvious place to set up a new life. Robert Sutton and his wife Sarah had never been made aware of Saville's past and readily agreed to him moving in to their house. For William there was

High Pavement, Nottingham today. The author

also an added attraction, Sarah's sister Elizabeth Tait who lived just a few hundred yards from the house in which he found himself living. Within a month he had become a regular visitor to her door and over the next ten weeks or so she began to believe in the possibility of marriage. All would have been well had not Ann walked in on the Sutton family on 20 May 1844.

After spending three months in the Nottingham Union Workhouse her sister had discovered her whereabouts and visited with the news that William was about to set up home with another woman. Ann left the same day armed with five shillings and sixpence, a mix of tea and sugar which she kept wrapped in paper in the pocket of her dress and a vague address. After making enquiries of any she met she was eventually directed to the Sutton household. Sarah Sutton, who met her at the door, believed her to be William's previous landlady and on that point Ann did not disabuse her. But the damage had already been done. Though William was able to convince Sarah that the woman she had met was all she believed her to be, he could not convince Elizabeth. She had been told by others who had met Ann that she was indeed his wife, had been left in the workhouse and furthermore, she was the mother to three of his children. When the two met that evening she told him in no uncertain terms to leave her house and not return. William was devastated, the secret life he had been slowly building was in serious danger of being destroyed by the woman he thought himself rid of. That night, still unable to accept the truth of his situation, he continued with the lie that Sarah Sutton still believed, adding that the reason behind the visit had been to collect rent arrears owed for storing his clothes. Sarah knew from a conversation between the two earlier in the day that he had only sixpence (2.5p) to his name, so paying any kind of arrears was unlikely to happen, but William insisted he would need to go into Nottingham next day. Sure enough he set out the next morning for the home of Samuel Wardle.

It was to the Wardle's that any furniture the Saville's owned when they agreed their split had been sent. It was also the place William knew Ann would go. He arrived at the house early in the morning. It was a warm day and, after waiting for Ann to dress herself, he told her he was going to take her and the children to

Carlton. They all left at around ten o'clock, William returning some three hours later in a somewhat agitated state. According to the story he told to Samuel's wife Lucy, they had never made it to Carlton having had a row two streets away. William said he had left them all outside Beardsley's shop (a place Lucy would have known well from the clock that stood outside) because Ann *'had turned nasty and would not go further.'* Lucy was dismissive and somewhat unbelieving. After a brief exchange of words he left. Nothing more was heard until he returned again between eight and nine o'clock that night, claiming to be concerned that his wife had killed all the children and thrown herself into the river. The Wardles were suspicious. The more upset William became at the thought of his wife having killed his family the more they suspected his involvement. After he had left the house Lucy lost no time in spreading the idea that it was he rather than Ann that had done the drowning.

When William returned the following morning (Wednesday) he found himself besieged inside the Wardle's house by women from the neighbourhood. So incensed were they at the prospect of having discovered a murderer in their midst the house was eventually surrounded and Lucy forced to send for police assistance. Samuel Wilkinson the local police inspector arrived to find a crowd he estimated at over one thousand. According to his later testimony, Saville was taken into custody for his own safety. On arrival at the local lock-up he was searched and found to have a small quantity of tea wrapped in paper and two shillings and a penny ha'penny. He was then questioned and placed in a cell whilst further enquiries were made.

On Thursday morning, 23 May, police felt there was sufficient suspicion as to the whereabouts of his family and his possible involvement in their drowning that they had him brought before the Mayor. He made a statement to the effect that he had not seen them since the argument outside Beardsley's shop and had spent the remainder of that day drinking in various public houses. There was nothing to add he insisted and the Mayor was likely to have agreed had it not been for a timely interruption. Whilst Saville had been giving his version of events, John Swinscoe had been staring down at the bodies of three children he had discovered inside woodland at Colwick; the body of a

Colwick Woods as they are today. The author

Colwick Weir where William Saville had intended to drown his family. The author

woman he found in grassland some four or five yards away. Within two hours they had been identified as Saville's wife Ann and her three children. The body of Ann Saville lay on her back with an open razor held in her left hand. Any hopes William had harboured of release that morning were obviously dashed by the discovery.

On Friday 24 May he was brought before Coroner Charles Swann to attend the inquest into the deaths of his family, held at the house of William Parr, police constable of Colwick. The bodies were housed inside an adjacent barn where they lay awaiting formal identification. This fell to William Saville, who, on arrival at the makeshift court, was first taken to see them as they lay beneath blankets on the barn floor before being brought into the house. After completing this formality, visibly upset and handcuffed to inspector Wilkinson, he was taken into the body of the house where the cuffs were removed and he was allowed to sit and listen to proceedings as they unravelled.

By the time the court had convened all traces of the murder scene itself had been obliterated. People had been arriving at the woods at Colwick since dawn, trampling the site, removing blood splattered plants or shrubs, stripping bark from trees and generally removing or destroying anything associated with the murder. So, when constable William Parr stood up to tell the court of the murder scene he had found, it was the only clear eye witness evidence they would hear. According to the testimony he gave, the children lay together as a group just inside the woodland. As he had already reported, some yards away lay the body of Ann Saville, still clutching the razor believed to have been used to carry out the killings. At first, he told the court, he believed she had been responsible and had afterwards committed suicide. It seemed a logical assumption to make in light of the available evidence. But he had also noticed that the tall grass around her body had been flattened in one long swathe leading from the children to the place in which she lay. In his opinion she had been dragged or pulled along the ground, which suggested a third party. The court was under no illusions as to who that third party was.

William Saville, a man of about five feet six inches in height with salt and pepper hair, having listened to the constable's evidence was asked by the coroner if he wished to ask any questions. In a faltering voice he declined. No doubt at that point he had realised how the day was to go and knew well enough why every eye in the room was upon him. The Wardles were brought into the court and reiterated the events surrounding Ann's supposed walk to Carlton, as were the Suttons who described in detail how Saville had reacted after Ann's visit to their home. Elizabeth Tait explained just how she had fallen for Saville's lies and her reaction to the discovery of his being married. But the damning evidence came from John Brown, a milkman. He knew the Savilles from when they had lived at Sneinton and at half past eleven on Monday, 20 May he saw the whole family walking down Colwick Lane. Everything William Saville had said up until this point was destroyed by this single testimony. The jury took fifteen minutes to declare wilful murder against him and he was ordered to stand trial at the summer assizes.

William Saville stood in the dock before Lord Chief Justice Denham on 2 August. Mr Wildman and Mr Mellor prosecuted on behalf of the crown and a Mr Wildman acted for the defence. Unlike the inquest there had been time to sift through the various pieces of evidence. It was quickly proved that on the day of the murders he had lied about his movements, that he had been in Colwick with his family that morning, that he had had opportunity. Further witnesses had been found to substantiate the milkman's story. People who had clearly seen the family walking by the woods and two young women who had actually spoken with the children and Ann Saville. It was irrefutable evidence and accepted as such by the defence who had decided from the outset not to challenge it. Instead, they argued that though Saville had lied he had done so out of fear. He had been made aware, so they argued, that Ann Saville had threatened to take the children's life. Concerned both that she would do so and that he would be implicated, he had simply panicked. There was a sense of guilt, they continued to argue, brought about because he had not stayed with the family that morning when he knew he ought to have done and he had lied for that reason. It may well have been an acceptable argument to the jury had it not been for inspector Wilkinson.

After Saville's arrest and before he had appeared before the mayor he had been searched. The results of that search began to form the foundation of the prosecution case. Police had found on his person two shillings and a penny ha'penny along with a quantity of tea. This they insisted proved his guilt. Sarah Sutton was asked to reaffirm the evidence she had given the coroners court as to the state of Saville's finances at the time he set out to meet his wife, that he only had sixpence to his name. Hariett Brownsword confirmed she had given her sister five shillings and sixpence along with a quantity of tea the day before she died and police confirmed that after examining Ann Saville's dress none of these items were found. The conclusion was obvious. If William had set out with nothing how had it been possible for him to be arrested with these items on him if he had not committed the murders and robbed his wife? It took the jury

The footpath through Colwick Woods near to where the bodies of Ann and the children were found. The author

fifteen minutes to agree. Lord Chief Justice Denham passed the only sentence available under law.

William Saville was sentenced to hang on Friday 9 August. Five days before this was carried out he was visited by Nottingham's prison chaplain, Reverend W Butler, no doubt to ask the man to atone for his sins. However, he found Saville in a rather garrulous mood and after carrying out the usual ministrations began to discuss with his prisoner the journey he had made that had brought him to such an ignominious end. After talking for some considerable time about his childhood, early work life and so on, the chaplain decide to write the conversation down at which point William Saville began to make a confession. Throughout the inquest and the trial he had insisted upon his innocence, now with death staring him in the face he had decided to set the record straight. But this was not to be the confession the Reverend would have expected. According to the statement he made and set his mark upon, it was true that he had gone to Colwick with his wife and children:

We went on by the Hermitage, down to this wood where I lay down a good while. I went into the close to ease myself, and left my coat for her to sit on, and the razor (that is my own) was in the coat pocket; it was the razor now in my trunk, black hafted. While I went to ease myself she went into the wood and called Mary there, and Harriet, saying 'Come in here till father comes back – be quick.' I heard her hard by; I was by the well...when I went back and into the wood, she had cut the throats of the two girls, and was in the act of doing the little boy, whom she finished. I heard Tommy cry and said, 'What's amiss with you?' She looked back as if she was wild. I said 'You brute, you bitch. I'll finish you an'all now. I took the razor out of her hand...I pushed her down backwards and kneeled on top of her, with my left knee upon her and the right foot by her side...I gave her a cut in the throat, but she sprang up backwards and fell down again twice...and then I went and caught hold of her head and gave her another cut, standing on her left side, which settled her at once.

The razor used to murder the children was certainly his, he explained, taken from his pocket by Ann. The razor found in his wife's hand he went on, had come from a man he had met some time ago in Southwell and was always kept by his wife for cutting her corns. Once he knew she was dead he had taken it from her, dipped it in the children's blood and placed it in her hand. He wanted it to appear as if she had used it to kill the children and herself. But by his own admission it would have been too blunt:

I never thought of using this razor. My real intention was to drown them and myself in Colwick weir. My prevailing motive was the misery of living with my wife. She said she would never leave me but follow me wherever I went...

The confession has a ring of truth about it and certainly Saville insisted for the remaining days of his life that it was an accurate version of events. Either way, it made no difference to the outcome. On 9 August William Saville took the short walk to the scaffold watched by a crowd numbering in the thousands. He had decided before mounting the scaffold that he would make no statement to the huge crowd. A huge disappointment to those who had gathered to hear the guilty man confess. But Saville insisted he would feel uncomfortable making any kind of speech and felt strongly the crowd would barrack him the moment he mounted the steps. He was right of course and the densely packed mob of sightseers roared their disgust as he took his place on the scaffold. Yet within minutes of the trap opening and Saville falling to his death it was they who were suddenly in danger of suffering the same fate. A cry went up to rush the scaffold steps with the result that twelve people were killed, trampled under foot as they tried to extract themselves from the dense, heaving mass, ensuring Saville's notoriety would be forever over awed by the infamy of his execution.

Chapter 3

The Price of Jealousy – The Murder of Ann Mellors 1877

At some time in 1873 Thomas Gray met and fell in love with Ann Mellors, an attractive twenty-seven-year-old living with her mother and younger brother. The family lived above a grocer's shop, which the two women ran together in the village of Car Colston. Thomas had been infatuated by the woman he had watched on numerous occasions pulling up the shutters every morning and setting out the shop window. Ann, on the other hand, felt less enamoured. Probably flattered by the attention she agreed to see him on odd occasions but never intended the relationship to be other than it was, in the main innocent. So when Thomas asked her to marry him toward the end of that year her rebuff was instant. Somewhat vexed by such a presumptuous proposal she also put a stop to their burgeoning friendship. Suitably admonished, Thomas retreated back into the heart of his family. To him it was a devastating denial of the love he had harboured for years; to Ann it was no more than an irritation. For her there had never been any kind of love match, so much so that apart from a passing comment made to her mother the same day it was never discussed again. As far as can be ascertained the two, despite living in the same village, kept to their respective ends of the street without ever meeting until 20 August 1877.

In the intervening four years Ann met and became engaged to Joseph Holt, the two had planned to marry the following year. Whilst Thomas on the other hand had become increasingly reclusive, suffering a variety of illnesses, the causes of which had proved increasingly difficult to diagnose, though in the main these illnesses seemed to affect his mind more than his body. According to his father, James, they caused his son to retreat ever further from the realities of day-to-day life, which in turn

View looking into Car Colston village, c.1910. Nottingham City Library

had a serious effect upon his physical capabilities. By early 1877, when he suffered some sort of seizure or fit, he had stopped helping to farm the thirty acres the family managed in and around the village, believing himself incapable of carrying out any kind of sustained manual labour. By the summer he had stopped sleeping, preferring instead to walk around the house until dawn. This in turn began to have a serious detrimental effect upon his father. Seeking out what medical opinion he could, he took Thomas to Nottingham to see a doctor Brookhouse, on 15 August 1877. His diagnosis was melancholia, for which he had no cure. Prescribing a drug to try and keep him calm, which was all he felt able to do, he sent the two men away with instructions to visit him again one week on.

Five days later, 20 August, Thomas, having slept much of the night, awoke around 5.30 am. According to his father, who had been up and about for a good half hour or so, he appeared quite rational. At about 6 am James Gray left his son in the house whilst he went out into the cattle shed to milk the cow. At the other end of the village John Mellors was just getting up. After opening the shops front shutter he walked to the bottom of the stairs and called his sister Ann to come down and open up. It was the usual routine of the day. Satisfied he could hear her moving around the bedroom he left the house and walked up the yard. Hannah Fretwell, who lived across the road from the shop, saw her sister at around a quarter past six walk out to the side of the shop and pull open a small shutter forgotten by her brother. Some fifteen minutes later Hannah watched again as Thomas Gray, a man she had not seen for four years, walked past the window of her house, crossed the road and pushed open the wicket gate that led to the side door of her sister's house. Upstairs, above the shop, Ann's mother Elizabeth heard the gate open and footsteps along the short path, thought nothing of it and continued dressing. At a little after 6.30 am she walked downstairs and into the shop expecting to find her daughter setting up for the day. But the shop was quiet; Joseph Holt heard his prospective mother in law first call out then scream. Running downstairs he found her knelt beside the body of her daughter, Ann, who lay on her back, behind the shop counter. So savagely had she been attacked that blood pooled across much of the floor from the large open wound in her throat. She was clearly dead. Lifting her, he carried her into the back room and laid her on a sofa. There was nothing either of them could do.

Thomas Gray meantime walked calmly from the shop, down the street and into the yard of William Clarke, his brother in law, in search of his sister, Lizzie. At the time William stood talking to Thomas's uncle George Gray, it was clear to both men immediately they saw him something desperate had just taken place. Thomas was covered in blood; it ran down his arms and soaked his trousers. Unable to comprehend what he was seeing, William grabbed him by the arm, dragged him into his house and locked the door. Sister Lizzie was still in bed so William pushed him into the bedroom. Thomas made no attempt to deny that he had just murdered Ann Mellors; he was apparently quite calm and perfectly lucid. Leaving him in the bedroom with Lizzie, William went out to find James Gray. After telling him of

Car Colston Common, 1929. Nottingham City Library

his son's confession the two men ran across the village to the Mellor's house where they found, as Thomas had said they would, that Ann Mellors had been murdered. Returning back to Clarke's house they tried to talk to Thomas and ascertain exactly what had taken place that morning. He was having none of it, other than admitting murder there was precious little else he would say. At a little after nine o'clock police constable Peck arrived at the house and took him into custody.

At a special court hearing held in Bingham on 27 August, Henry Wotton, surgeon of the parish, gave the first real clue as to what had happened that morning. According to his testimony Ann Mellors had in all probability been attacked from behind and, because the wound that killed her had been made to the left side of her neck, whoever wielded the razor found at the scene had been right handed. Further examination made the day after Ann's body had been removed from the house revealed she had sustained ten distinct cuts. It was the first cut however, which Dr Wotton believed had resulted in her death. He told the court that this cut had penetrated so deep as to sever the spinal cord that death would have been instantaneous. All the others, though in themselves life threatening, had in his opinion, been the result of frenzy. It was doubtful, he added, that Ann Mellors had ever really been aware of her assailant until he was behind her and then it would have been too late to prevent the attack. After listening to other witness evidence the special hearing charged Thomas with wilful murder and he was placed in custody to await his trial at the winter assizes.

The trial opened on 31 October before Mr Justice Hawkins, Mr Etherington-Smith acting for the defence, Mr Mellor QC for the prosecution. From the outset it was the defence intention to prove insanity. There was no doubting Thomas Gray had committed murder, since his arrest he had never denied it. The question the defence counsel intended to put to the jury was simply, did Thomas Gray know what he was doing at the time? Obviously if they could place enough doubt into the minds of the jurors then they stood a reasonably good chance of winning the day. It was not to be an easy question to answer.

Dr Brookhouse, whom Thomas had met with some five days before the murder, was of the opinion that melancholia, which he had diagnosed was a form of insanity. Furthermore, he told the court that he was also of the opinion that it could lead to delusional tendencies, which in turn brought about homicidal mania. If that happened, he argued, then these feelings of homicidal mania would inevitably bring about a sudden attack of violence which would be perpetrated on any person, no distinction being made between friend or foe.

Dr Phillimore, medical superintendent of the County Lunatic Asylum at Sneinton, added further corroborative evidence. Having met with Thomas whilst he had been incarcerated in Nottingham prison he too had formed the opinion that the man suffered from melancholia. He sited the fact that Thomas had left his murder weapon, a cut throat razor, at the scene of the killing, as confirming Dr Brookhouse's diagnosis that this same melancholia had indeed turned into homicidal mania. Discarding the means of carrying out a murder at, or in the

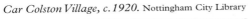

Car Colston Village, c.1920. Nottingham City Library

Car Colston, Notts.

vicinity of the body was classic, he argued, in that type of mental derangement. At the time of the murder, according to Dr Phillimore:

> *...he could not control his thoughts or regulate his conduct with safety to himself or others – that his mind was disordered, and that he did not therefore know the difference between right and wrong.*

Mr Etherington-Smith had by this time begun to create doubt. Insanity he continued to insist throughout the day, was a symptom suffered by Thomas Gray and had definitely contributed to the murder he had carried out. He used the two doctors' evidence to ram home the point that the condition was one, which the defendant had suffered from for years, but that it had only been over the summer months this same condition had evidenced any serious deterioration:

> *This man has received in some way an injury to the brain, which had produced the mischief, which had left him in the opinion of the doctors whom he had called subject to paroxysms of mania, so that he was dangerous to himself and others...He was not acting as a sane and brutal murderer would act when he made nine gashes on the throat of the unfortunate woman, after destroying her life by cutting her throat from ear to ear.*

It was a compelling argument and no doubt one received with some sympathy by those sat in the courtroom. Unfortunately for Mr Etherington-Smith it was not a view shared by those who had spent the previous eight weeks sharing a cell with Thomas Gray.

Joe Hardy and Charles Gray (no relation) told the court that the defendant had told them not only of his guilt but also of the charade he had made feigning insanity. As far as they were concerned he was guilty of murder. Dr Isaac Massey, surgeon for the prison, tended to agree. In his opinion no delusional signs had been exhibited whilst under his care. He had, he testified, discussed the murder at length with Thomas and apart from claiming not to have been aware of his actions he offered up no explanation. Ann Mellors had died as a result of her refusal four years earlier to marry him.

Mr Justice Hawkins agreed, informing the jury during his own summing up that there seemed little evidence to convince the court that Thomas Gray had not understood his actions on 20 August. The guilty verdict when it came some few minutes later was as expected.

George Balk who had acted as solicitor for Gray immediately mounted a petition for his reprieve. He argued strongly that the killing was motiveless, that Gray had never pursued Ann Mellors once his marriage proposal had been rejected, therefore it could not be argued that he had killed her for this very reason. That the prisoners who testified he had talked of insanity as though he had invented the whole condition to evade conviction should never have been allowed to testify in court and finally that homicidal mania had been proved. It had merit and found some support amongst the lawyer classes but not with the Secretary of State. It was rejected on 19 November and the unfortunate Thomas Gray was executed at eight o'clock on the morning of 21 November 1877.

Chapter 4

For the Sake of Money –
The Trumpet Street Murder
1885

For almost nine years Elizabeth Williamson had lived a lie. Since the age of twenty-three she had promoted the idea amongst those who knew her that she was a married woman, an essential status to hold in Victorian society if you were to live with a man. But James Tucker, the man whose name she had taken would have no truck with marriage. To him marriage was an anathema, something to be avoided. Throughout the relationship he had insisted on remaining single despite Elizabeth's protestations. It was something she came to accept and quite possibly appreciate as the years went by. But when they moved into a tiny terraced house near Sneinton Market in the summer of 1876 it was something to keep to herself.

From the outset the relationship was often difficult. Tucker could be violent when under the influence of alcohol. Neighbours reported arguments, many of which often resulted in punches being thrown with the unfortunate Elizabeth being on the receiving end. But these same neighbours also knew she too was no angel and would often precipitate these outbursts herself after a night spent in the pub, goading Tucker into violent rages. By the early 1880s she had begun to find solace in a bottle. This in turn increased the tension in the house, which inevitably increased the likelihood of violence and eventually led to her being imprisoned for assault. After serving three months she returned to Sneinton but the relationship by this time was probably beyond redemption.

In March 1885 they moved to a house in Trumpet Street, possibly to be near her father for added support. Any pretence at being married had been dropped by this time, her new neighbours being aware from the day they arrived as to the standing of their relationship. It mattered little to either of them. Tucker had become quite open about his disgust for Elizabeth, beating her regularly. She in turn continued to drink. Neither harboured any illusions as to their future together. Recognising no doubt the futility of their situation, yet at the same time, in an almost perverse way, being accepting of it.

On Saturday, 9 May, some eight weeks after the move the situation came to a final and devastating end. Tucker and Elizabeth had been drinking with a friend, Henry Emerson in the *Horse and Trumpet*. It had been a long night and this was the second pub they had been in since early evening. There was no doubting the fact that both were a little the worse for wear. At around half past ten that night she bought the last of several rounds of drink and after finishing off her half pint left the two men in the bar to walk the short distance home. Tucker stayed

The house in Trumpet Street. Steve Jones, Wicked Publications

on until just after eleven o'clock, bemoaning his luck to his friend Emerson and damning Elizabeth for still being with him. Emerson in turn accused him of being too violent and told him he should leave her before it got any worse. But Tucker was in no mood to leave her, not at that point anyhow. Returning home the inevitable row started immediately he walked inside the house, this time instigated by him. He was angry, frustrated, depressed and drunk. At some point in the fight that followed he knocked her to the floor, took a stone bottle containing paraffin, poured its contents over her, struck a match and set her alight.

Across the road a neighbour, William Savage, saw fire through the front window of the house, running across the street he forced his way in and found Tucker standing over the now fiercely burning Elizabeth. Unable to do anything to douse the flames he screamed out for help. This brought a second neighbour, John Dykes who had been in his own yard, filling a bucket with water. Using this to extinguish the flames the two men between them managed to save Elizabeth's life. Tucker, according to evidence they were to give later, stood by the fireplace and looked on disinterestedly, occasionally shouting out at them to leave her: 'Let the ****** burn.'

Hearing all the commotion, Henry Emerson, only too well aware of Tucker's mood after leaving the pub, came into the house just as Tucker began to lash out again at Elizabeth, this time with his boot. Horrifically burnt, Elizabeth by this time was barely conscious and totally unable to protect herself from the continuing onslaught. Seeing this, Emerson quickly stepped across her, shouting at Tucker to leave her be. But he was too far gone with rage. The two men grappled and Emerson, being the sober of the two, eventually got in a blow that knocked Tucker to the ground. With him silenced he scooped Elizabeth in his arms and carried her to the General Hospital.

When constable Brown arrived at the house, having been brought by William Savage, it was after midnight. Tucker was still in a state of rage and shouted his innocence to any as would listen. Refusing to leave the house he claimed Elizabeth had thrown an oil lamp at him but its contents had fallen across her skirts and set her alight. He was not the guilty party here, he insisted. But the police constable was an observant man. While

Tucker, still crazed with anger continued to rant, he ran a knowledgeable eye about the room. On the corner of the mantle shelf behind Tucker's gesticulating body he could see the only lamp in the room still intact, whist on the floor lay a stone bottle without its top and a spent match. Stooping to pick up the bottle, he recognised the smell of paraffin and, according to his later statement, knew without asking that Tucker was lying. It took further police help and a serious scuffle in the front room of the house to get him out onto the street. Only at that point did Tucker resign himself to the inevitable.

On Sunday, 10 May medical opinion was such that the injuries sustained by Elizabeth were deemed so serious that her chances of survival were virtually non-existent. Alderman Barber J P decided it prudent to visit her and record what he considered would be her dying deposition. Tucker had been charged with assault but everyone involved in the case realised this was likely to change to murder, but if the charge was to have

Taking Elizabeth Williamson's Dying Deposition. Steve Jones, Wicked Publications

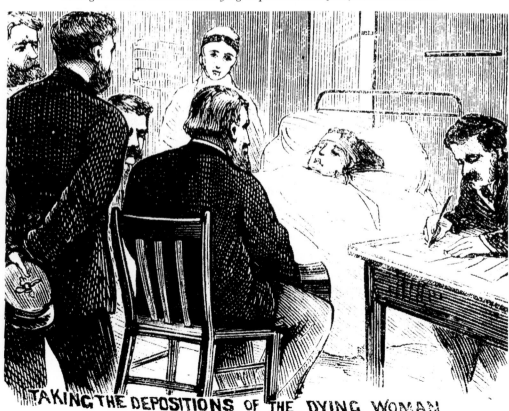

any realistic chance of conviction then Elizabeth Williamson needed to record her version of events. To comply with the law of the day Tucker had to witness this statement being taken and so was brought to the hospital from his cell. For Elizabeth, conscious, in considerable pain and aware of her perilous situation, this must have proved extremely difficult.

The small party of legal men, Tucker and her treating doctor, gathered around the bed mid-morning to hear and record every word the woman had to say. Arduous as that meeting must have been for all concerned Elizabeth nevertheless gave a version of events that fit the evidence found by the police. According to the statement she made, Tucker had kicked her to the ground before pouring paraffin over her and setting her alight, but even on the point of death she insisted she believed he had not been aware of his actions. Tucker said nothing throughout the short meeting and after being returned to prison was charged with unlawful wounding. This changed to murder after Elizabeth's death on 15 May.

The Coroner's court held at the hospital on the following Monday heard evidence from all those involved but it was police evidence that damned Tucker more than any other. After their arrival at the house and the brief but violent scuffle to force him out of the room in which he had burnt Elizabeth, they told the court that he had offered up no mitigating circumstances, showed no signs of contrition and exhibited disappointment at being told she still lived. He was recorded as saying in answer to the question as to whether or not she was dead that, 'If she is not, she ought to be.'

It was this hostile attitude, despite a change of heart on the Sunday he attended hospital, that convinced the court not only of his guilt, if that had ever been in doubt, but of his intent. There was no doubt in the minds of the jurors having heard the police evidence that James Tucker was not only culpable but also guilty of murder.

The trial opened on 14 July 1885. It was, as expected, short and decisive. Tucker, who by this time had been discovered to have used two aliases over the past few years, stood in the dock as Joseph not James. He appeared calm, as he had done throughout his incarceration. Though it is doubtful he ever

Narrowmarsh, 1913. Nottingham Public Library

envisaged being found not guilty. The prosecution case was straightforward; he had committed murder they claimed by setting fire to Elizabeth Williamson as a result of an argument. It was undeniable and Tucker had no sustainable defence for his actions. Though having obviously given a deal of thought over the intervening weeks since the coroner's hearing to his earlier claim that it was she, not he, who had thrown a lamp which caused the fire, and recognising the futility of such a claim, he changed his story. After listening to the witness evidence that had first been aired some two months earlier the defence began to argue strongly in favour of manslaughter.

Aware from the outset that it was pointless attempting to show he could not have carried out so heinous a killing they decided a plea of drunkenness in mitigation could remove the spectre of the gallows. It was probably the only defence option available. It could also have proved successful had it not been for the violent history of the couple. This in itself obviously showed to the jury that he had displayed periods of violence in the past, coupled with his recorded anger immediately after the attack, manslaughter had little chance of being successfully proven.

In his summing up, the Judge viewed the idea of this being manslaughter somewhat sceptically:

If the only defence were that the prisoner was drunk, however reckless from drink he may have been when he committed this crime, I am bound to tell you that that forms no defence whatever. Because if a man chooses voluntarily to place himself in a condition of brutalised drunkenness so that he becomes irresponsible in one sense for his own acts, whatever may be the view taken from a moral point of view, the law can only deal with men according to their act; if a man chooses voluntarily to place himself in a position of drunkenness and then takes away the life of a fellow creature or does any other act, he cannot plead that drunkenness as an excuse.

The jury concurred and after a twenty minute deliberation returned a verdict of guilty of wilful murder.

Despite attempts to have this sentenced commuted to life the verdict was upheld. The Secretary of State rejecting the final appeal on 31 July. Tucker, who had probably never harboured any thoughts of his sentence being commuted to life, made no act of contrition. He had known that his guilt had been clear from the moment of his arrest. On Saturday, 1 August Berry, the executioner and one time member of the Nottingham police force, arrived in the city to supervise the necessary preparations. Three days later, at eight o'clock in the morning, Tucker made the fateful walk to the scaffold, which had been erected in the yard of the Nottingham Gaol on St John's Street. It was a bright summer morning, a bank holiday and the city was teeming with people heading off to catch early trains for the coast. For most people Tucker's execution had been forgotten but for a small group who gathered outside the prison gates there were prayers to be said. A silence fell as the clock chimed out the hour followed by a muted buzz of anticipation as the black flag was slowly hoisted and then, breaking into small groups, the crowd began to disperse. For them justice had been well served.

Chapter 5

The Strange Shooting at Hyson Green
1893

William Smith was an inventor of note. For much of his life he had dedicated himself to the textile and allied industries where he invented machines for use in the manufacture of gimps and beaded trimmings for ladies dresses. After his marriage to Harriett during the 1850s this interest was expanded to incorporate the manufacture of pleated cord, and, by 1860, his voracious appetite for things mechanical had led to a key invention in the manufacture of chenille. As his family of three boys and two girls grew he moved away from textiles, transferring his expertise to heavy industry where the rewards were anticipated to have been greater. Here he developed and patented a machine capable of producing a product we today know as wire netting. Produced originally in Manchester and Warrington, its successful use in Australia to prevent rabbits destroying crops had sealed its reputation and had he been able to manufacture the netting himself, these rewards would have been significantly enhanced. But William Smith was never considered, by those who knew him, to have been wealthy. Quite possibly for him the invention and the journey he had to take to make it was what gave him the greatest satisfaction. In later life this boundless enthusiasm for things new he brought to the bicycle industry. Recognising the growing trend he saw around him, a need for his skill he set up his own manufacturing company, investing both time and money in an enterprise he hoped would secure his financial future. Unfortunately he died, insolvent, before that vision could be realised.

It therefore fell to his three sons to pick up the mantle he left behind and continue where he had left off. But only Walter, who had worked alongside his father for the last years of his life, had the inventor's disposition. He set up in Abbott's Factory, Hyson

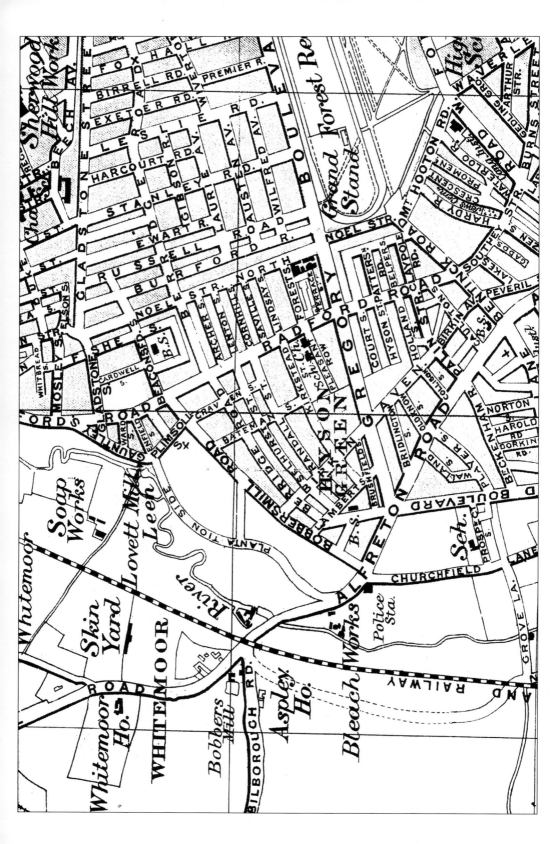

Green, where his father had worked and where other manufacturers shared various floors and outbuildings. Success was slow to come but after a few years his continued work in the area of ladies fashion had begun to pay dividends. This in turn led him to refine his father's process for manufacturing chenille and by 1893 he had perfected, invented and patented a machine capable of producing this as a coloured fabric. Considered a major breakthrough by the textile industry, the machines he built were eagerly sought out and his future looked assured. But in December of that same year something was to happen that would destroy forever both his fledgling company and himself.

Catherine Cross was a very attractive twenty-four-year-old woman who had often visited his mother to have dresses made. In early 1892 she had moved from Nottingham to take up a position in Liverpool's women's hospital as a nurse. Because of the distance involved she restricted her visits home, only returning to Nottingham when she could take a holiday. At the end of November 1893, with Christmas looming, she managed a two-week break and arrived at her parents' house on Saturday the 25th. Whilst living away for the previous eighteen months or so she had met and become engaged to a young man from the hospital. Part of the reason for the visit home had been to introduce this man to her family and arrange the wedding. Unfortunately, for Catherine, pressures of work had kept him in Liverpool and prevented his travelling down until the following Saturday, so she took advantage of the time alone to catch up on old acquaintances and friends.

On Tuesday, 28 November, she arrived at Harriett Smith's house to have measurements taken for a new dress. Having not seen her for some time Harriett invited Catherine to stay for tea. Glad of the company she readily agreed. At around five o'clock that night Walter, who had continued living with his mother after his father's death, arrived at the house and joined them. Neither knew each other well, passing acquaintances no more. But during the course of tea a semblance of friendship developed as Walter became more and more animated about his latest invention. Harriett encouraged the conversation and as tea concluded asked Catherine if she had any interest in bicycles. Ever polite she said she did but that her knowledge was limited.

Walter, suddenly aware of a potential convert, began to tell her of his father's interest and how he too had become an avid enthusiast, inviting Catherine to return on the following Thursday in order that he could take her out on a tandem he had developed. She was more than a little reticent at the suggestion, no doubt concerned for her own safety. Being evasive she made no definite arrangement. Using other commitments as an excuse, she said she may not have the time but would try. Walter, seemingly unperturbed, asked if she would go over to the factory on the Saturday morning and allow him to show her the new chenille machine. By this time in the afternoon he knew she had arranged to meet her fiancè off the twelve-thirty Liverpool train, the factory was en route. Whether through courtesy or kindness, she agreed. At around eight o'clock with tea long since over and Catherine eager to be away Walter did the gentlemanly thing and walked her the short distance from the house to Hyson Green cemetery. Here she met, as she had arranged to do earlier in the day, with her sister Lizzie. Reminding her of the arrangements the two had made he then left and returned home.

By Thursday, Catherine's enthusiasm for bicycles had waned somewhat and she failed to make the afternoon appointment she had agreed to. Calling instead in the early evening for a brief chat with Harriet, Walter, vexed she had not taken up his offer of a ride on the tandem, gave her a somewhat cool reception, her excuse of family obligations grudgingly accepted. She left reaffirming her intention to still visit the Abbott's factory on the coming Saturday and agreed a time of 10 am.

What Walter decided to do next was never to be fully explained. On the following Friday at a little after one o'clock in the afternoon he walked into Jackson's gun shop on Church Gate. Explaining to bemused shop assistant, John Wigley, that he needed to purchase a revolver but obviously had no knowledge of how they worked. Wigley proceeded to show him a number of different weapons, explaining their operation and showing Walter how they were to be loaded and fired. Making his choice he paid £2 for the gun, bought an additional one hundred cartridges and left. On returning home he told his mother, without showing her the gun, that he had decided to invent a mechanism that would enhance a revolver's firing capability. After eating, he returned to his rooms on the upper floor of Abbott's factory, set up a variety of boxes as targets and spent the next couple of hours teaching himself the rudimentary art of marksmanship.

At seven o'clock the following morning, much earlier than his normal practice, he was back in his machine room ostensibly to prepare for Catherine's visit, returning home in time to meet her when she arrived at ten o'clock. But she was in no such hurry. Having stayed in bed longer than she ought and then having possibly forgotten her arrangements on time, it was nearer 11 am when she knocked on Harriet Smith's door. Walter invited her in and after the usual courtesies were over he walked her the short distance to his factory. Numerous witnesses saw them arrive at a little after 11.20 am and watched as the two climbed the staircase, on the outside of the factory, to the upper floor where Walter unlocked the door and took her inside.

What happened over the next one and a half hours has remained shrouded in mystery. What is known is that at around one o' clock in the afternoon Walter produced the revolver from his jacket pocket and, pointing it at Catherine, said – 'your money or your life' – not believing him to be serious she put her hands to her face in mock horror but Walter then shot her. The bullet struck her right hand, deflected, and then passed through her chin, into her neck, down her windpipe and shattered onto her spinal column. Dazed, frightened and obviously disbelieving of what had just happened, for a moment she just stood as if rooted to the spot. Walter calmly asked her if she had been hit, she said she had and as if then suddenly aware of the danger of the situation she was in, she turned away from him and ran. Forcing the lock off the door through which they had both entered the workshop she ran for the stairs. At this point Walter fired two more shots, neither hit her, then reloaded the revolver and threw it into an open tray of cultivated mushrooms covering it over with a piece of sacking.

Catherine, after reaching the bottom of the steps, ran out into Forest Street, collapsing beside the iron railings of the first house she came upon. A crowd quickly gathered. From a vantage point at the top of the factory steps Walter Smith could clearly see and

Forest Street, Hyson Green in 1961. Nottingham Public Library

hear the growing commotion. At that point his choices were simple. Either run to where she laid declaring his innocence and proclaiming some sort of dreadful accident or ignore it and go home. When he met an excited Edwin Cope, manager of a hosiery company sharing the same building, at the foot of the stair, he had already decided upon the latter. Edwin, having heard the commotion, but not the shots, had already been out into the street when the two men met. Declaring to Walter as they passed each other that a woman had just been shot Walter gave back a disinterested *has she?* and walked off in the opposite direction. It was a comment that he would later regret.

For Catherine it was not so simple. After being carried, still conscious, into the house outside which she lay she was examined by a Dr Tibbles who confirmed the self-evident diagnosis that she had been shot. Unable to carry out anything other than the most rudimentary first aid there was little else he could do but wait for a horse cab to take her to Nottingham's General Hospital. Police in the shape of Sergeant Aldridge, officer in charge of the Hyson Green area, arrived before she was carried away and conducted a reasonably thorough interview. Catherine, breathing with difficulty but showing no outward signs of distress tried to explain what had happened to her some five minutes earlier. Informing the sergeant that it had all been an accident, that Walter Smith had not intended the gun to go off. Conscious of the need to preserve the scene as best he could and not accepting of Catherine's story, he sent two constables back to the factory to ascertain the truth of the matter. As he left in the cab with her for the short journey to the hospital constables Willoughby and Sumner were climbing the steps that led into Walter Smith's machine room.

According to their later testimony they found the lock on the door leading into the workshop to have been broken off, two spent bullets around the area of the stairs, a revolver, two boxes of cartridges and various bullet holes or marks around the inside of the walls. After some discussion between the two officers it was decided to leave Sumner to detail the findings whilst Willoughby made his way to Walter Smith's home at 210 Alfreton Road. When he arrived it was to find both Walter and his mother were out. Unruffled and obviously believing Smith would return he waited. Sure enough at a little after three o'clock that afternoon Walter walked back into the house and was promptly arrested.

Just where he had been was no mystery. Shortly After Catherine's arrival at hospital both he and his mother arrived, unbeknown to police, at her bedside. The three of them had a conversation lasting fifteen minutes or so witnessed by nurses but not overheard. According to statements made later they

Nottingham General Hospital. Author's collection

simply wanted to check that Catherine was all right. They insisted no pressure was intended or applied to ensure she would corroborate Walter's version of events. Either way when Justice of the Peace, Mr Acton arrived at the hospital late on the Saturday evening, having been informed of a deterioration in her condition, it was to find that she did just that. According to her deposition there had been no argument, falling out or attempted assault, the gun had simply been aimed and fired accidentally. She could offer no explanation as to why or how two further shots had come to be fired at her.

Thorough examination of the machine room during Sunday revealed that over the course of two days, Friday and Saturday morning Walter had fired thirty cartridges which made it nigh on impossible to be able to say with absolute certainty that when these other two shots had been made it had been intended they hit Catherine. But the evidence of the two bullets on or around the stairs was enough to suggest this had been the case and as a result he was duly charged with attempted murder. He appeared in a special session of the magistrate's court on Monday, 4 December. All this changed however when Catherine, after undergoing a tracheotomy operation to alleviate severe breathing difficulties, died in the early hours of Wednesday morning.

The inquest opened the same evening in the hospital's boardroom and concluded on the 15 December. During the second session it became apparent, despite her claim of an accidental shooting, that the police were developing a case centred around a possible assault against Catherine Cross, arguing that Smith had lured her there on a pretext. Why, ran the argument, would a woman who had no known knowledge of, or interest in, textile manufacture spend so much time inside a workshop where the only article of note was a chenille machine? As they unravelled the circumstances surrounding the shooting they laid more and more emphasis upon this single fact, claiming she would not have intended to miss her fiancè's train, which was due to arrive at Nottingham station at twelve thirty that afternoon. Enough evidence existed to show that visiting the workshop was only an aside, something she had agreed to do out of politeness because it lay on her proposed route that morning. Why, they went on, would she have remained inside Abbotts factory until almost one o'clock unless something untoward had taken place? In support of this assertion they produced the dress she had worn on the morning she had been shot, torn across the right hip, a position they insisted that could not have been accidental. But the most damning testimony came from doctor John Gray, medical officer at the general hospital. He told the coroner's court that shortly after her admittance Catherine gave him a version of events at odds with the version she later gave in her deposition:

She said that without any cause he fired at her. She turned and ran, and he fired three more shots after her. That was her statement. She was in a conscious state at the time and fully knew what she said... she said that she thought the first shot was an accident, but she hardly thought so after hearing the other two shots.

Hyson Green Cemetery. The author

Other than a discrepancy as to the number of shots fired it took the jury no more than twenty minutes to return a *wilful murder* verdict.

Walter Smith appeared before Mr Justice Hawkins at the Nottingham Assize Court on 6 March 1894. The prosecution produced witness evidence throughout the day to show that in their opinion Walter Smith had concocted the notion of an accident hours after the shooting had taken place. Arguing strongly that having not tried to assist Catherine after she lay in the street was almost proof positive that he had intended murder when he fired the revolver. Gun experts were produced to show that the shots could not have been accidental; a fourteen-pound pull being required on the trigger meant the gun would never have fired unless intended. Therefore, ran the claim, if the first shot had not killed her then the follow up ones were intended to do so. Returning home was no more than a reflex action, something he had done since childhood. He wanted his mother to sort out the mess and put things right. Attending the hospital was an attempt to do just that and led directly to Catherine's deposition supporting the accident theory. But the tear found on her dress and the fact she had missed her fiancè's train, were powerful pieces of evidence, which lent credence to the fact that she had not told the truth. Why, was pure conjecture. Perhaps, they reasoned, she had not wanted to embarrass herself or Walter's mother Harriett, who she had known for a number of years. Either way, Walter had bought a gun, a revolver, a weapon he had had no previous knowledge of and had spent much of the day before her visit teaching himself the rudimentary skills of handling, loading and firing it. Nothing, they insisted, happened accidentally.

It was powerful stuff, leaving the defence with little room for manoeuvre. So they pursued the only legitimate and credible line of argument available to them, motive. There was none they asserted. The two people had only met five days earlier; there was no evidence of any previous association and none that would indicate any future association. Catherine Cross had known from the minute she had been admitted into hospital that she had been the victim of an accident and made her deposition to that effect without coercion. So brief and unintended an involvement between what were essentially strangers could not have resulted in murder.

Equally powerful but not believed by the jury who returned a guilty verdict. Mr Stanger, who conducted the defence immediately set about drafting a petition for reprieve based upon two keys facts not aired at the trial. He claimed that shortly after Catherine Cross had been carried from the street she was taken to the home of Mary Simmons, a woman she had never met but who attempted to give first aid whilst they waited for Dr Tibbles to arrive. Whilst this was ongoing Catherine had made a statement in the presence of a second woman, only recorded as Mrs Greenwood, which would have shed a different light upon the events of the morning of the shooting. This evidence had been ruled inadmissible because it had not been a dying declaration.

The petition, which carried an attachment bearing nine thousand signatures from people who believed Smith to be innocent, was rejected on 22 March. There was nothing else he or his family were able to do. Twenty-four hours before his execution they all gathered for the final time. Smith continued to insist he had not deliberately fired the gun and that the whole wretched incident had been an accident. Thousands obviously agreed. By early morning of 27 March they gathered outside Bagthorpe prison, lining the roadside, four deep in places, beside the iron railings. The *Nottingham Daily Express* likening their numbers to those of a football crowd. It made little difference to Walter Smith who became the first of fifteen executions at Bagthorpe over the next fifty years.

Chapter 6

The Lincoln Street Tragedy – Mary Rose 1896

John Rose was fifty-two-years-old when he moved into 1 Islington Place, Lincoln Street, in the early part 1895. Up until this point he and his wife Mary had been happily married. No one would have ever suspected this apparently idyllic relationship was about to change. Everyone close to them thought them to be an extremely happy couple that, despite their frugal lifestyle, had managed to build a strong marriage. All knew the house move was of necessity, since John worked as a baker and Mary had to leave the house every morning at seven o'clock to start work in the lace industry. For years this had meant long days with little time left for each other. They needed to be nearer the city. If John Rose had never lost his job perhaps this is how their lives would have turned out, but he did and from that point on nothing would ever be the same again.

In November 1895, as part of a general downturn in Nottingham's fortunes, workforces were being cut back. In turn this had a knock on effect on other industries and John Rose found himself unemployed. Despite his best efforts through the early winter months he could find no work and in turn no replacement income for the one lost. The overall result of all this was an unwarranted financial pressure on the two of them. Living in a household where every penny had its place, removing the higher wage earner was bound to have an impact. Christmas came and went with no relief in sight and as January dawned what had begun two months earlier as niggling arguments were now full blown fights.

Unable to cope with the pressures, Mary took to drink and before the month was out had been imprisoned for being drunk and disorderly. John was incensed. Possibly he felt betrayed by

Nottingham market place, c.1910. Author's collection

her conviction or by the sanctuary she had sought through the bottom of a glass. Either way after her release from prison there was a palpable escalation in the intensity of the rows between them. Neighbours began to talk of the sounds of violence they had heard each night and the shouting that went on for what seemed like hours. Though no one ever saw Mary marked or bruised in any way. Possibly because they had grown more aware as the months went by that out of the two of them it was often she who had exhibited the more destructive nature.

On the night of 11 February, a week or so after John had discovered his wife had not been paying the rent, things came to a head. They had an argument, not about the arrears but about which of their few possessions they were to hide from the bailiffs due on the following morning. The disagreement led to a very loud, angry and near public exchange which lasted from half past eight that night until just after nine o'clock. Alice Young who had befriended Mary and lived at the opposite side of a shared yard found a distraught Mary at around half past nine stood outside her house crying bitterly. The two women talked for some minutes, Alice offering what support she could including a room for the night if Mary needed it. A not unusual occurrence over the past few weeks, but Mary seemed comfortable enough and after regaining her composure returned home.

At a quarter past eleven that same night another neighbour, Ellen Duckworth, whose house faced the Rose's across this same yard, saw John Rose stood just inside his doorway. He appeared agitated and seemed to her to be looking for his wife or at least glancing up and down the yard. She watched unobserved until he closed the door and saw the light in the downstairs room disappear and reappear in the upper room as John carried an oil lamp through the house. All the houses in Islington place were three storeys, each level consisting of one room. In the Rose household the middle room they used as a bedroom, so as far as Ellen Duckworth was concerned he had gone to bed.

Nothing disturbed the neighbourhood for the rest of that night. At eight o'clock next morning, as was her usual custom, Alice Young walked the short distance across the yard and turned the handle of the Rose's back door to let herself into their house. She and Mary normally walked to work together; it was usual to find a fire lit and a light burning. If they had the time the two of them would have a chat over a cup of tea before setting out. But when Alice turned the door handle that morning it was to find the door still locked. Knocking brought no response so she went to fetch her nearest neighbours. They in turn hammered on the door and called to the upper window. Realising after a futile attempt to force the door that something was seriously amiss Alice had someone fetch the police. Constable Porter, known to everyone locally, was there within minutes, after some further unproductive shouting he attempted

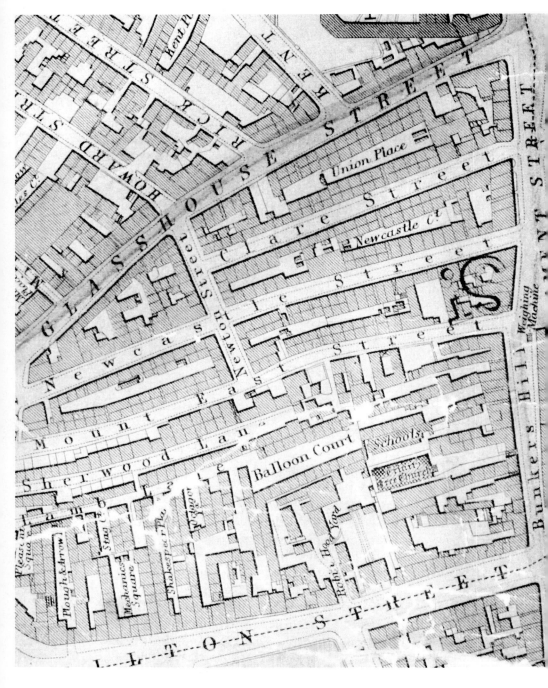

Extract from Salmon's map of 1861 showing Lincoln Street (off Clumber Street).
Nottingham Public Library

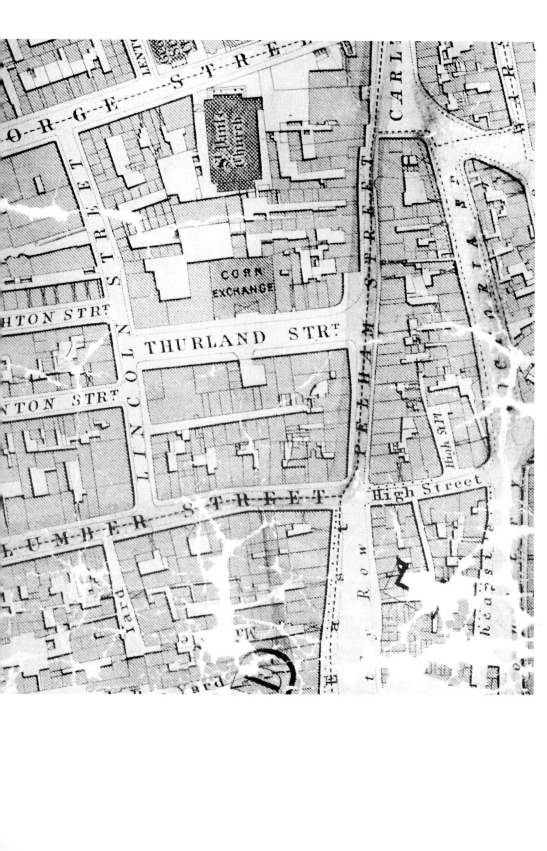

to rouse the house using a clothes prop on the bedroom window. With no response and fearing the worst, he too decided to emulate the earlier attempts at forcing the door but met with the same fate. Undaunted, he had someone fetch John Harrison, the local joiner, while the assembled group of anxious neighbours stood around stamping their feet in the early morning cold until he arrived.

It took the joiner no more than a few minutes to gain entry and by eight thirty both constable Porter and Alice Young were feeling their way up a darkened staircase. As the policeman pushed open the bedroom door they could clearly see, in the light from the uncurtained window, two bodies. John Rose lay on his back with his feet under the bed but obscured by much of the bedding, which appeared to have been pulled from the bed. A savage cut had laid open his throat and most of the blood from the wound had soaked into the front of his nightshirt, he was still alive. Mary lay beside him, face down, her left arm behind her back, several wounds to her neck and throat and clearly dead. The bed, devoid of its covering, was saturated in blood indicating that the violence which had taken place inside that room had probably started there. After ushering Alice out of the house constable Porter was joined by his sergeant and the two men organised a doctor to tend John Rose.

Dr O'Mullane examined John Rose where he lay, in a semi-conscious state, and found the wound to his throat looked worse than it actually was. The cut had not severed any major artery and the lack of haemorrhage had not only saved his life but, in the doctor's opinion, had also enabled him to move around after it had been inflicted. For the two police officers stood in the bedroom it indicated that they need not look outside the house for the attacker. Checking doors and windows and finding all either locked or tightly fastened added credence to growing idea that John Rose had murdered his wife and attempted suicide.

As they lifted Mary from the bedroom floor they found a knife beneath her right arm, which subsequent examination proved to be the murder weapon. It had inflicted terrible injuries on her hands, which Dr O'Mullane believed to have been defensive injuries and had severed the jugular vein in her neck. The latter he believed had been the last wound made and had obviously been responsible for her death. As he examined her he found in all some ten different cuts, four, which he found around her throat and face in his opinion were life threatening.

Police were satisfied by late morning that John Rose, for whatever reason, had attacked Mary whilst she slept. Superficial wounds indicating that a struggle had taken place on the bed and that at some point the two of them had struggled violently on the floor of the room. Probably they had rolled off the bed, which was why the bedding had been found around their feet, but that it seemed Mary had attempted to stand up and reach the door. Post-mortem examination confirmed doctor O'Mullane's earlier diagnosis as to the fatal wound and added the rider that this same wound had been struck from behind. Damning for John Rose who, according to all the available evidence, had been the only other person in the house that night.

At his trial before Mr Justice Grantham at the Crown Assize Court at Nottingham's Shire Hall on July 23, John Rose disputed this interpretation, insisting that whilst it was true no one else had entered the house it was not true that he was the perpetrator of a murder. Accordingly he pleaded not guilty. Ably defended by Mr Dominick Daly who had spent much of the summer studying the case, his defence was that it had been Mary not himself that had gone to bed that night with a knife, and her intention had been to commit suicide. He, ran the argument, had been unfortunate enough to awake whilst this was going on and the ensuing struggle to stop her taking her life had unfortunately precipitated the opposite result but only after she had attacked him, cutting him badly across his throat and rendering him unconscious. Had it not been for good forensic detail it might have been a contest he would have won. As it was the trial became a courtroom conflict centring upon the evidence of three eminent doctors.

Dr O'Mullane, who spent one and a half hours in the witness box, maintained his composure and insisted his original diagnosis concerning the wounds found on Mary Rose was consistent with that of the post-mortem. The wound that killed her had been struck from the centre of her throat and extended back beyond her right ear, it could not, he argued strongly, have been self-inflicted. Mr Dominick Daly was adamant that the doctor's opinion was not only wrong but wholly prejudiced, formed after entering the bedroom and finding the body:

> Have you come to this case with a strong feeling in your mind that the man had murdered the woman? Is not that the reason you think the man inflicted the wound on his own throat?

The doctor insisted he had not; that only the evidence he had found had influenced his thinking and the evidence he claimed was clear.

Dr Herbert Taylor who had assisted at the post-mortem heaped more misery upon the defence. He agreed with Dr O'Mullane, a wound severing the jugular as deep and as long as that found upon Mary Rose could not, be believed, have been self inflicted. So when Dr Robert Hogarth, the man who had treated John Rose at the hospital, took the stand to say that the wound he had found in Rose's throat must have been self inflicted, so the cut being transverse, a sure indicator suicide had been attempted, not oblique which would have supported the notion of an attack, the defence was lost. Despite a valiant speech to the jury in which Mr Dominick Daly contended that of the two only Mary Rose had exhibited a tendency toward violence, that she had been imprisoned for drunkenness, had a violent temper and was of a build that would have made it difficult for any such attack to have been made against her with any certainty of success. The jury disagreed, after an adjournment of only ten minutes they returned with a verdict of guilty. John Rose was duly executed on 11 August 1896.

Chapter 7

A Family Squabble – The Shooting at Hickling 1899

In a moment of sheer madness fifty one year old Elias Torr wrecked the lives of the family he had spent thirty years building. It was an act of unmitigated violence they would all forever regret and an act he would pay the ultimate price for committing. But thirty years earlier it had all been so very different.

Born in Old Basford in 1848, Elias had trained as a butcher, a skill his family believed would see him through life. Apprenticed from an early age, it became a trade he felt comfortable with, something at which he excelled. In the early 1860s he took all these skills north and moved into Leeds. Here he began to create a name for himself amongst the locals as a man who only sold good quality meat. It was a reputation he was proud to own and when, in 1869, he met and married Ada, the two of them decided to move back to Nottingham and open up a butcher's shop. Over the next thirty years they ran a number of shops in villages around the city whilst bringing up a family of two boys and four girls, growing reasonably prosperous in the process. This prosperity in turn allowed them to expand their horizons. So when in 1896 an opportunity arose for Elias to take on a farm at a small hamlet known as Hickling Pastures, he had no hesitation in seizing it. Here he farmed sixty acres beside the Melton road, some eight miles south of West Bridgford, mostly pastureland but with some small acreage of arable whilst at the same time maintaining an interest in properties in Basford.

But all was not well in the Torr household. Those who knew the family knew also of Elias's growing dependence upon alcohol. For over twenty years he had been a heavy drinker and by the time of his move to Hickling had already been warned by

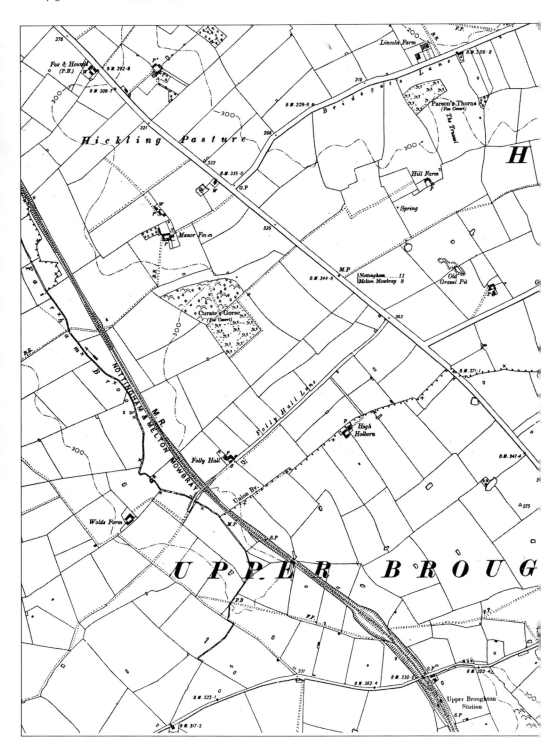

Ordnance Survey Map of Hickling Pastures, 1901. Nottingham Public Library

his doctor of the inevitable health problems that lay in store should he refuse to desist. The family though feared more than just a decline in his health, although there were two healthy sons who could take over the running of the farm were it necessary. What caused the greatest amount of consternation were the mood swings. When Elias Torr took to drink he became a violent, uncontrollable man who became capable of indiscriminate violence. For his wife and children, brutality was usually aimed at them, followed by a visit to the pub. By 1899 it had become a commonplace event and they had grown to expect it.

Unfortunately for Ada both her sons had married and moved out of the farmhouse by this time, which she felt had left her more vulnerable to his unpredictable rages. It was always she who bore the brunt of any anger he brought back from his drinking bouts and it was she who had to protect as best she could the four girls that remained at home. Though the eldest of this group, twenty-seven-year-old Mary Ann had begun to assume a shared role with her mother as time went on. Where she could she would use her position in the ranking list of her fathers affections, which she knew to be high, and try to act almost as a buffer between the two. It had its successes and her growing reputation as an evangelist preacher had begun to help her confidence grow so that she felt better able to withstand the blast of anger that sometimes walked in through the front door of the house.

Unfortunately for her though, on 1 May 1899, she found herself caught up in a maelstrom brought about by Elias Torr's inexplicable belief in his wife's infidelity. All total nonsense but after five hours spent in the *Fox and Hounds* on Melton Road his grasp on reality had been severely diminished. At a quarter to five that evening he pushed open the farm door and launched a tirade of abuse directed at his wife. Incensed, Mary Ann immediately jumped to her mother's defence and managed to prevent Elias striking out with his fists. But frightened and aware of what was likely to happen if she stayed, his wife grabbed the younger children and simply ran. Mary Ann, recognising the same signs as her mother, followed on behind. A field away lay the cottage home of William and Kate Doleman, the nearest

Farms at Hickling Pastures today. The author

refuge to the farm and the little group had no hesitation in heading for it.

Elias, well aware of where they would go, made no rush to go chasing after them. He wanted retribution, but wanted it his way. In the kitchen was a single barrelled shotgun used by his eldest son for scaring off birds. It had been loaded the previous day for just such a purpose and left where it was easily accessible. This Elias lifted from its mountings. Without further ado he calmly walked from the farmhouse and up the field to the Doleman house. At the garden fence he paused for a minute or two calling out to his wife, telling her to come home. When that met with no response he threatened to shoot her if she stayed where she was and pushing open the garden gate walked up to the front door of the house. By this time his wife along with the youngest child, ten-year-old Ruth, had already escaped through the back door. Unaware, Elias used the butt of the shotgun to break through the panels of the door, determined if she was not to come out then he would force a way in. Meanwhile, Mary Ann, who had not run out with her mother, stood just inside the house's scullery shouting at her father, calling him a devil, telling him to leave, go back to the farm. Elias ignored her and pushing the barrel through the opening he had created he fired a single shot. The bullet hit her in the right arm and chest breaking two ribs and killing her instantly.

Elias was distraught, pushing open the shattered door he knelt down beside the body and wept. Others ran for help, they did not have to run far, the sound of the gunshot brought men running in from the fields and within the hour constable Keeton from Kinoulton arrived to take him into custody. Elias made no attempt at escape and during the journey to Bingham told the police constable he had killed his daughter:

My daughter came to the door and said something she ought not to have said. I pulled the trigger and it was done in a moment.

The inquest opened at Torr's farm on 4 May. Surgeon Edward Trevor told the hearing that the gunshot had penetrated the heart; Mary Ann never stood a chance from the minute Elias fired. He also expressed an opinion that in order for the shot to have hit her as it did he must have held the gun to his shoulder before firing, damning for Elias because it suggested he had deliberately aimed, that the shot fired was intended to hit whoever stood in his way and that whoever stood there he must have seen. Whether or not he knew it was his daughter in front of him was immaterial, so ran the argument and the jury agreed.

Shire Hall. The author

Whilst this was taking place, family and friends were arriving at Torr's farm to attend Mary Ann's funeral. It had been agreed that she would be interred in the family grave at Old Basford. So from early afternoon people had begun to travel in from the surrounding villages, particularly Widmerpool where much of the family had settled. Others travelled into Nottingham by train to meet the courtège as it passed the station, which it did at around four o'clock in the afternoon. Up until that point, its progress into Nottingham had gone largely unnoticed. It was only as the growing line of mourners reached Sherwood Rise that people began to gather on street corners until finally a crowd of several hundred lined the last mile or so of its route.

Two months later, on 20 July, the trial opened at the Shire Hall. In the intervening weeks and despite Elias's apparent disinterest, a defence of accidental shooting had been carefully pieced together. On oath he contended that when he approached the Doleman's house that evening he had no intention of killing anyone. Furthermore, he insisted that when he pushed the barrel of the gun through the broken door he could not see if anyone stood the other side. It was a reflex action to fire but it was accidental, not an aimed shot.

Mr Etherington Smith disagreed. He insisted that the killing had been deliberate. In his opening to the court he had told Mr Justice Lawrence, presiding, that when Elias had returned from the *Fox and Hounds* public house on 1 May it was to find his wife providing tea for a farm servant named Tom Thornton. This was the man Elias Torr believed to have been having an affair with his wife. The argument that followed his arrival home had been caused by this man's presence. But, he maintained, after Mrs Torr and her daughters had left the house Elias did not immediately give chase. Instead he waited for Tom Thornton to finish his tea, he was calm, had nothing to say, there was no abuse made of the man. It was some time later that he went into the kitchen of the farmhouse to take down the gun. Here Tom Thornton's evidence proved crucial.

Taking the stand he told the court that there were two guns kept in a rack on the kitchen wall. One a single barrel, muzzle loader, which required a cap on the nipple before it could be discharged. That gun had been loaded after having been taken out by Elias's son Alfred on the Sunday but the cap had been left off when it had been replaced back in the rack. The other was a breech-loader. It was the first gun, the muzzle loader that Elias took down and carried across to the Doleman's house.

Widmerpool church. The author

A man named Samuel Dalby added corroborating evidence. He had not only seen Torr walking across the field that night but had joined him in the walk, the gun was being carried in his left hand and from the conversation the two men held it was evident he intended to do harm. As far as he could tell the gun was primed for use.

From these two pieces of testimony alone Mr Etherington Smith showed that when Elias Torr left his fireside that night with the muzzle loader he had replaced the cap else he would never have been able to fire it; if that were the case, ran the argument, then he had certainly intended to use it. If he needed more to show intent it came from William Doleman who had stood in the kitchen of his own house and watched as Torr shattered the panels of his front door. From his position in the room it seemed to him that the man had to have had a reasonably clear view into the scullery. So large was the hole punched through the door that at one stage he reached in from the outside and tried to turn the door handle, had the door not been locked he would have been through it, as it was he had to have seen his daughter and certainly heard her.

When, having listened to all this, Elias Torr finally took the stand in late afternoon it must have seemed like a lost cause. Yet he insisted, as had been decided prior to the trial, throughout his testimony that he had never intended to kill anyone on that May Day. He had, he insisted, taken the gun from the kitchen to shoot birds. Walking across the field to the Doleman house had been an afterthought, no more. Only once he stood outside did he decide to go and force his wife to go back home. The gun at that stage, he agreed, was not set to fire but held at half cock and unnecessary, but once he reached the house it seemed reasonable to make some sort of show with it. But his intention was only ever to scare her, make her see reason, get her and the children to go back to the farmhouse with him. When he fired he did not fire with the intention of killing Mary Ann. The gun, he claimed went off by accident.

Had it not been for the testimony of gunsmith, Samuel Jackson who owned a gun shop in Church Gate, Nottingham, his argument may have won supporters, but Jackson had a contrary view to that expressed by Torr. According to his testimony the gun used was in bad condition and if fired at half cock it would not go off.

Mr Justice Lawrence in his summing up saw this as crucial and damning to Torr's claim that he had fired accidentally:

Mr Jackson stated that he had several times tried the effect of pulling the trigger when the gun was at half cock and in no case did it explode the cap...if he fired a gun across the court and killed one of the people there it would be no good him saying he had no ill will towards the person killed. It was said that if any injury was intended in the present case it intended to the wife, but even if that were so the law was plain that if a person shot at someone and killed somebody else with the shot the person shooting would none the less be guilty of murder.

The jury took twenty-five minutes to agree and Elias Torr was sentenced to death, the execution taking place on the morning of 10 August at Bagthorpe prison. A curious crowd of over one thousand gathered outside the prison, standing in subdued silence as the prison clock struck the hour of eight, dispersing only after the hoisting of the black flag signifying sentence had been carried out.

Chapter 8

A Question of Insanity –
The Matthews Murder
1905

Twenty-nine-year-old John Hutchinson had spent much of his life alone, whether as a result of upbringing or some sort of mental illness is not known. Certainly he was born into a family that suffered greatly from the latter. The year before his birth his uncle, John Norman, committed suicide by cutting his own throat. Eight years later John's son Thomas hung himself. This was followed by a second hanging in 1892 by another uncle, this time his father's brother William and then by two of his aunts who decided to commit suicide by drowning, one in the river at Carlton, the other at Burton Joyce. Not the most auspicious start to life, particularly when added to the list, was two other family members, both committed to mental asylums during the latter part of the 1890s.

As a young man he often would disappear from home for days on end, telling no one where he went to and always alone. The older he became the more these frequent disappearances were tolerated, though quite possibly they were no more than escapism. Daily life for the Hutchinson's could best be described as grinding poverty. The family were poor, his father scratching a living where he could, money was scarce, at times non existent. For John, growing up in this environment must have been a bleak experience.

At twenty-one he was involved in a serious accident that would add further problems to an already desperately unhappy life. Run down by a horse cab, he was badly kicked around the head and back before being trampled beneath the horse's flailing hooves. As a result he began to suffer from fits, never fully diagnosed, but believed to have been epileptic in nature. Withdrawal became a way of life. Slowly he drifted

Narrowmarsh, a bird's eye view in 1919. Nottingham Public Library

toward alcohol, which brought relief, of a kind, and became more and more introverted in his outlook. After suffering a series of fits during 1896 he left his job as a collier and began to work as a general labourer wherever he could find employment, never staying in one place for too long. By the winter of 1904 he had taken up lodgings in a place known locally as Chapman's

Yard, Malt Mill Lane, Narrowmarsh, a notorious slum consisting of mainly tenement housing, situated just outside the city centre. Here he stayed until December when, having lost his job as a platelayer on the Midland Railway, he decided to enlist. Joining the Notts and Derbyshire (Sherwood Forresters) Regiment just before Christmas that year, he began training at Normanton Barracks. It was to be a short-lived career. After some six weeks the army had had enough of him and he was discharged as unsuitable toward the end of January 1905.

Homeless, he returned to Narrowmarsh, one of Nottingham's worst slums and to George and Rose Matthews with whom he had lodged before his disastrous move into the army. They were only too willing to have him back. Short of money and knowing Hutchinson had always paid for his board on time, it was an easy decision. It was also a catastrophic one.

Then Matthews had a son, four-year-old Albert, about to celebrate his fifth birthday, a little boy John Hutchinson was comfortable around. Rose Matthews had a job working at the nearby laundry, which necessitated her being out of the house for periods of the day and early evening. George, having been long term unemployed, spent much of his time hunting down work, so having someone who could look after the child whilst all this was going on had become a real need. Hutchinson, being out of work and therefore free to take on the role, was a heaven sent opportunity to both of them.

On 31 January, a week after his discharge from the army, he had agreed to return to the house at five o'clock to put Albert to bed. Rose had arranged to be home by around eight o'clock, so Hutchinson was to wait for George's return before going out again, as had become normal practice. After a day spent drinking he was somewhat the worse for wear when he walked into the *Millers Arms*, which then stood near to Chapman's Yard. George Matthews, who had walked into the pub minutes earlier, and knew Hutchinson should have been home, looking after his son, met him at the bar. The two men had a brief conversation and George sent him home to sober up, though he said later in evidence that the man was only, a *little fresh*, a colloquialism for less than drunk.

When Hutchinson arrived back at the house he found Albert

Narrowmarsh, c. 1920. Nottingham Public Library

in boisterous mood, too much for him to handle at that point of the day. After trying to quieten the child, which had little effect, he resorted to violence. Whether because of a threat or not is unclear but Albert grabbed a poker from the hearth and struck out. Hutchinson's reaction was extreme. Forcing the boys head back he began to choke him. As the child lost consciousness he took a knife from the kitchen and viciously slashed at the boy's neck until he had severed the head. Kicking the head under a sofa he then set about mutilating what was left of the body, eventually discarding it in front of the fireplace and returning to the *Millers Arms*. He walked back into the pub at around half past six. George Matthews was still stood at the bar, the two men exchanged a few words, Hutchinson ordered a pint of beer and said he was off to see his sister who had been ill, and he left at about seven o'clock.

An hour or so later Rose Matthews lifted the latch to the back door of her house and walked in on a scene of utter carnage. Unable to believe that the body lying by the fireside was that of Albert or that he had been murdered she ran screaming into the street convinced he had been burnt to death. Neighbours Thomas Rourke and Joseph Heap, hearing the commotion, ran into Chapman's Yard and broke through the door to get into the house. What they found would haunt them for the rest of their lives.

John Hutchinson meanwhile, having obviously realised he had nowhere to hide away, calmly walked up to the first policeman he saw and surrendered himself. Constable Tuxford, who escorted Hutchinson into custody, had no idea of the murder at the time he made the arrest. Only after the two men had walked back into Malt Mill Lane and met with Detective Superintendent Parnham, who had been fetched to the house, did the awful truth dawn. Hutchinson was taken to Leen Side Police station where he was formally charged with murder and later taken over to the Guildhall.

He never denied nor showed any signs of remorse for the murder. When he came before Mr Justice Phillimore on 9 March 1905 his defence, ably led by Dr Taraschand, entered a plea of not guilty on the grounds of insanity. In the circumstances the only option available to them and an option which must have been considered to have had some validity. After listening to what witness evidence was available Dr Taraschand set about trying to prove that Hutchinson, because of his family background and the injury sustained some eight years earlier, had to have been insane at the time he carried out the attack. It was to prove a difficult defence to mount.

Dr Herbert Taylor, who had been responsible for examining both the murdered child and John Hutchinson, expressed the opinion that insanity was not present either before or after the murder. Having interviewed Hutchinson at length he insisted nothing had come to light that would support the suggestion. According to his testimony Hutchinson had detailed the murder in his statement, showed no remorse, been fully aware of the consequences of his actions and expressed no regrets. Sufficient evidence, he argued, to prove insanity did not exist.

Dr Taraschand remained unmoved; he outlined the family history and told the court that this alone gave rise to the notion that insanity, if it existed within the Hutchinson family, as it clearly did, had passed down through generations to John Hutchinson. Epilepsy, he argued, exasperated an already volatile character, turning the man into a killer. Dr Thomas Goraty, physician and surgeon supported the diagnosis. According to his testimony he had formed the opinion that the circumstances of the crime coupled with Hutchinson's antecedents added credence to the fact that when he carried out the murder he had been suffering from epileptic mania. Furthermore, he insisted, he would only have emerged from this condition some hours later, his surrender to constable Tuxford being a clear indicator that this had been the case. This was corroborated by Dr Edge of Basford who, having interviewed Hutchinson whilst in police custody, added that the mutilation, which followed the killing, was also indicative of this type of insanity.

Had it not been for two key witnesses who disputed this mental assessment the case for Hutchinson may well have been won. As it was, the whole idea of some form of insanity was totally destroyed by Dr Powell, medical superintendent of the

Narrowmarsh during its demolition in the 1950s. Nottingham Public Library

City Asylum. His medical expertise in this area of science was enough to blow a hole through the defence mounted by Dr Taraschand. When that evidence was underpinned by Dr O'Kell, medical officer of Bagthorpe prison, under whose observation Hutchinson had been for five weeks, there was no going back.

In his summing up Mr Justice Phillimore expressed the view that not only was insanity a difficult condition to prove it also had to fit certain criteria:

> *...that a man was sane if he knew the nature and quality of the act, if he knew it was morally wrong. In other words it must be proved by those who put forward the plea that he was so insane that he did not know the nature and quality of the act he was doing... in cases where crimes were perpetrated by epileptic maniacs they were not conscious of what they had done... in this the man remembered practically everything. There was no evidence that the prisoner had shown any clear signs of insanity...*

The jury took twenty minutes to agree with these points and find John Hutchinson guilty. Henry Pierrepoint hanged him on 29 March 1905.

Chapter 9

A Deadly Affair –
The Canal Street Murder
1906

Edward Glynn could never have been described as handsome, most would have said that age had been less than kind, perhaps because he had spent a deal of time at sea his face had taken on a care worn look or perhaps he had simply had a hard and unlucky life. Either way, at twenty-six years old he was to be feared by those who knew him. Violent by character and mean by nature he was nevertheless a man of his word.

In January 1906 he met Jane Gamble, a woman of similar age. They drank together and by early February had moved into a house at Prospect Place, Leen Side, a slum area where poverty and disease were endemic but where Jane had spent much of her young life. The relationship was far from successful, Glynn requiring only the slightest provocation to lash out with his fists and Jane's life soon became a constant round of beatings. Fiercely jealous, he excused the violence as necessary to those that dared question the brutality, blaming Jane, pointing to what he thought were her various infidelities. Whether true or not Jane desperately needed to escape the house and some three weeks after having agreed to live with him she ran away. Arriving at her friend's house, Emily Day, in the early hours of 16 February, distraught and terrified she would be found; Emily and her husband Arthur hid her in the cellar. She had been severely beaten, her arms a mass of bruises, her face battered. All three knew Glynn would be out searching for her. Emily promised her Glynn would not get into the house, she was as good as her word. Crouched on the cellar steps she and Emily heard Arthur Day, an hour or so later, refuse to allow Glynn through the back door. Angry at being denied what he considered his to do with as he would, Glynn said when he

Leen Side, 1920. Nottingham Public Library

found her he would, 'cut her heart out.'

For the next two weeks Jane kept her distance but in Leen Side it was difficult to disappear. Lodgings were all she could afford and affording them meant she would always be within reach of the man she now desperately feared. There was little choice, as by late February she had taken up residence in a house Glynn could see from his front window and on 28 February he came calling. Though this time he was calm and collected, determined to get Jane back by guile, telling her he had changed, that all would be normality, no more beatings. She was disbelieving of the new man and told him after hearing him out that she would sooner drown. Glynn left, but he was not about to fade with the day.

By 1 March, as a result of the constant watch he had maintained on Jane's new lodgings, he believed she had begun to see a man named Henry Gibson. Enraged by jealousy, he had taken to pacing the pavements outside, determined she would know of his presence and unflinching in his resolve to do her some sort of serious damage. Belligerent and openly indignant to those who dared challenge his presence on the street, he made no attempt to hide the bitter resentment he felt inside. Jane was going to suffer and he wanted everyone to know it.

On Saturday, 3 March at around 11 pm all this anger finally exploded. Jane and Gibson had spent the night drinking and were walking back to their lodgings. As they approached Canal Street Glynn, unseen by either of them, stepped out of the shadows and plunged a knife deep into the back of her neck. The force with which he struck her broke the blade in half, over two inches of steel being embedded into her spine. Instantly paralysed down the left side of her body, her legs gave way and for the first time Gibson became aware of the attack. Grasping at Jane as she fell to the ground he saw and recognised Edward Glynn, the man who had spent so many hours watching their house, a man whose identity he could not have failed to realise. Leaving Jane, he gave chase along with a man named Richard Dixon who had just walked out of the *Lincoln Arms* and had seen the attack. But Glynn knew the back streets well and had disappeared into a labyrinth of alleys and side streets before they could get anywhere near him. Jane meantime had been found by the local beat bobby PC Aubrey, she was clearly dying, her breathing shallow, speaking only with great difficulty. She told him Glynn had attacked her, though she could never have seen him and gave Glynn's address. She died the following day.

At twenty minutes to two on the Sunday morning PC Aubrey made his arrest. Glynn, by now somewhat the worse for wear through drink but still well aware of all that was happening denied the attack. When charged the following morning with her murder he insisted he had spent the previous night in various

Extract from Salmon's Map of 1861 showing Leen Side and Narrowmarsh. Nottingham Public Library

pubs in and around Bulwell, contending that he could not have walked from Leen Side to Bulwell and back and have committed the murder. Unfortunately for him he could not find any witness to back up his movements.

He appeared at the Nottingham and Notts Assizes before Mr Justice Walton on 17 July. In the intervening four months or so he had not changed his plea, still defiantly adamant he had not murdered Jane Gamble. This, despite being picked out from identity parades by the two men who clearly saw him, albeit at night, after the stabbing. Edward Glynn, contrary to some expectations, was not about to make life easier for the Gamble family. He maintained throughout the trial that at the time the murder had been committed he and Jane had already settled their differences, that as a consequence he had no reason to kill her. The two hours spent together earlier in the day she died had quelled the anger of the previous week. No one believed him, no witnesses were able to testify to having seen the two together in cosy conversation, nor could the court accept that jealousy so deeply felt could so easily have been discarded.

According to the testimony of Mr Kenneth Black, house surgeon at Nottingham's General Hospital, it was only after Jane

Canal Street today. The author

had died that it was discovered the knife, or a rather a segment of it, was still lodged in her back. Post-mortem examination revealed the two inches or so that had broken off had remained embedded in her spine and had severed half the spinal cord. She could never have survived, part paralysis putting too much strain on her breathing, her body being unable to cope with such trauma, death he told the court, had been inevitable. Whoever had made the attack had done so deliberately, intending to kill or at least maim.

Glynn fitted the bill. He had all the traits in his character that would have enabled him to have made so desperate an attack upon Jane Gamble, claimed the prosecution. He had been clearly seen stalking her in the days leading up to the murder. Two independent witnesses had seen him commit the stabbing and had identified him as the killer. The manner of her death, the force by which the knife had been driven into Jane's back, both indicative of rage or anger, and the fact that Glynn was known to have been harbouring such an anger made it impossible for him to escape a guilty verdict.

Mr Campion, however, acting for Glynn's defence, had a different view. He argued forcefully that there was no basis in fact for this idea. He insisted that though a variety of witnesses were able to testify as to Glynn's apparent threat, the fact he had been clearly seen outside her lodgings had also verbally abused the woman and had told others of his intent to harm her, all meant very little. Everyone used threats at some time or other, he contended, but that did not mean these same threats would ever turn into real violence. It was a logical argument and one the judge felt ought to be well considered by the jury. In his summing up he told them that amongst what he considered to be the working class of Nottingham threats of the type outlined in the court were common:

> ...it was, unfortunately, common for people of this class to make use of violent and often beastly language, and utter threats which they had no real intention of carrying out. The jury must not, therefore, necessarily jump to the conclusion that because he made use of threats he was guilty.

They may have had sympathy with the view but were not about

Above and below: two Edwardian views of Nottingham's famous Market Square.
Author's collection

to accept it in Glynn's case.

It took fifteen minutes to decide he was guilty of murder. From the dock it appeared the verdict had been long expected. Despite requests from his counsel he refused to allow any petition for reprieve to be mounted, accepting his fate whilst still proclaiming his innocence, which he did stoically until the day before his execution. Only during an interview with his solicitor twenty-four hours before the sentence was to be carried out did he finally confess his guilt, acknowledging that when he had said to Arthur Day months earlier 'he would cut her heart out', he had meant it.

According to the *Nottingham Evening Post* in their edition of 7 August 1906, having conducted himself throughout with great indifference and having made his final confession, he met his death 'with calmness and equanimity'. There were no huge crowd scenes outside the prison. A crowd of no more than one or two hundred of the curious expressed any interest in Edward Glynn's final moments, standing in silence as the prison bell struck four times to signify sentence had been carried out.

Chapter 10

A Family Affair – Murder at Arnold 1909

Samuel Atherley had served in India and had been amongst those of Lord Frederick Roberts' victorious army when it entered Pretoria during the Boer war. Returning home in 1902 after an attack of enteric fever cut short his military career and forced him back into civilian life after nine long years. Having few skills, he worked for a while as a bricklayer but spent long periods in unemployment. In 1904 he met Matilda Lambert, unmarried, with a young four-year-old son, John. The two decided to live together and by 1905 Matilda had given birth to a second child, this time a daughter, Annie. Despite being the father of two children Atherley found it hard to settle. This in turn led to serious arguments in the house and by early 1906 Matilda had walked out.

The sister, Sarah Watson and her husband John gave her a bed. Over the years they had grown accustomed to the knock on the door late at night and had never turned her away. But from this point on life was to become more and more difficult for all of them. Samuel Atherley, for whatever reason, had begun to believe Annie was not his child. Whether or not Matilda had done anything to help foster this belief is unknown but certainly Atherley had begun to accuse her brother in law openly. What's more he cared little for who knew about his beliefs. Relationships were strained.

But by the following year they were back together again and Matilda pregnant with her third child. She eventually gave birth to a son, Samuel, named after his father. For a while they seemed content but as she had realised many months earlier, life with Atherley was unpredictable. He was a depressive, a man prone to long sullen periods during which he became either argumentative or withdrawn. He needed careful handling if the two of them were to remain together. Patience was not something Matilda possessed in any large amount, however. No doubt frustration at their lack of money and his constant refusal to find work proved a potent combination, too potent for Matilda to withstand for long. Inevitably, her dissatisfaction at his apparent indolence led to another split, possibly also fuelled by his growing antipathy to her first-born, John. Since the two had first met Atherley had mistreated the boy. This had begun to escalate as the years went by until, by the time Matilda ran away for the second time, she had become all too well aware that her son had been living in fear of his step father for some time.

How long they stayed apart on this occasion is not known but over the next twelve months they reunited and parted twice more until in May 1909 Matilda left, for what should have been the final time. Taking lodgings in Robinson's yard, off Front Street, Arnold. For three weeks she and the children lived alone but by the end of the month Atherley had forced his way back into the house. Despite Matilda's protestations he refused to move out and within weeks surrounding neighbours began to hear the sound of raised voices with an ever-increasing regularity. Atherley's jealousy knew no bounds, not only had he again begun to question Annie's paternal origins but had also become convinced Matilda had embarked upon an affair with a man named John Shelton, a man he knew to live nearby and who he had only ever seen as a passing acquaintance in the street.

As July dawned things began to take on a more sinister twist. Matilda, having refused to leave the house despite all these accusations of unfaithfulness, believed she had convinced Atherley that it was he who ought to move. She told those close to her that he had agreed to sell his things, raise a little cash and go. In the same breath, so to speak, she also said he had begun to sleep with a razor under his pillow at night. It was this last point that raised a great deal of understandable consternation amongst the neighbours living in the same yard. They wanted her to call in the police, have Atherley bound over, forced out of the house. But Matilda would have none of it. She insisted it was all a sham, that he would never use it or threaten her with it. It was a decision that would cost her life.

At a little after ten o'clock in the morning, 10 July, Thomas

Scene of the tragedy. Nottingham Evening Post

Marriott, who lived near to Robinson's yard, saw Atherley stood at the window of the upstairs bedroom. He was tapping at the glass as if to attract attention. Marriott ignored it, well aware of the man's eccentricities until, probably in frustration, Atherley punched his fist through the pane and beckoned to him for help. According to his later testimony it was clear from where he stood in the street that once the window had been broken he could clearly see Atherley had been bleeding heavily from his throat. Running into the yard at the back of the house, calling for help as he went, he made for the back door. After a few fruitless attempts to break in Atherley turned the lock from the other side and let him in. Covered in blood and still bleeding from a serious gash across the neck he was unable to talk in anything but a whisper. It was enough to tell Marriott in a series of gesticulations and garbled words to go upstairs. Fearing the worst he made his way gingerly to the only bedroom in the house. Inside were two beds, pushing open the door he could clearly see Matilda Lambert in the first laying with her son Samuel, opposite in the other lay John and little Annie. All had been covered over using coats, the family had never owned blankets, and from the amount of blood pooled around each bed all were clearly dead. As he pulled back the coverings it became obvious their throats had been cut.

Police were on the scene within minutes, and found the murder weapon with its blade broken inside the bedroom fireplace. Examination of the bodies at the house was carried out by the local GP, Harvey Francis. He was of the opinion after a cursory examination that more than one weapon had been used. All had serious head wounds none of which could have been made using a razor. A search of the house revealed a large coal hammer, short shaft with a spiked head. This corresponded entirely with the wounds the doctor had found and Atherley, still downstairs whilst all this was going on, agreed he had used it. He indicated with his fingers that he had carried out the murders at 3 am. Satisfied, police had him taken to hospital believing he would not survive the wound he had inflicted upon himself during a failed attempt at suicide.

That same afternoon an inquest into the killings was opened at the Public Offices in Front Street. Coroner Parkinson heard evidence as to cause of death and the deterioration of the relationship between Matilda Lambert and Samuel Atherley that led up to it. It took no time for the jury to bring in a verdict of wilful murder. If Atherley survived his injuries he would stand trial for the killings.

Survive he did and the trial duly opened on 12 November before Mr Justice Pickford. When he stepped into the dock there was little sign of the terrible injury the cut throat razor had made to his neck. He spoke clearly, giving a firm *not guilty* in answer to the charge of murder. Four months of rest and recuperation had brought him back to health. But it had not provided an adequate defence. Atherley arrived at the court without representation of any kind. Despite his long recuperation no one it appeared had seen fit to appoint defence counsel. Justice Pickford refused to allow the case until proper consultation had taken place, instructing a Mr Hadfield to act on Atherley's behalf and put the trial back to mid afternoon to allow what he considered sufficient time for this consultation to take place.

When Mr Ryland Adkins KC, MP got to his feet to open for the prosecution, the light already beginning to fail outside. The court, however, remained crowded, mainly by women, many of whom had taken their seats earlier in the day expecting a morning start but had stayed on after the postponement. They listened in silence as he outlined the facts behind the killings, of how Matilda Lambert had tried in the past to leave Atherley and of the history between the couple. There was little doubt, he insisted, that Atherley was a jealous man who was perfectly sane when he took a razor to his children and their mother. Insanity, the court by this time knew, was the only defence Atherley's counsel had been able to mount. But no evidence existed to support the argument. Mr Ryland Adkins wanted to ensure the very idea was not to be entertained throughout the course of the trial. The list of witnesses taking the stand that afternoon ensured that it did not happen.

Police constable Lomas told the court that after his arrest and whilst being taken to hospital Atherley had made a statement,

Front Street, Arnold today. The author

albeit with some considerable difficulty. In it he had said that he had killed all the family at three o'clock in the morning using the razor found in the fireplace; the razor had broken as a result of the attack so he had been forced to resort to a second razor in his own attempted suicide. He made no mention of a hammer. Dr Francis however most certainly did. He told the court that all the victims had been beaten about the head using the coal hammer found at the house before their throats were cut. The intention obviously to render them all unconscious thereby making it easier for Atherley to complete the murders using the cut throat razor. None of which the defence counsel contested. What they wanted to know was whether or not Samuel Atherley had been aware of his actions when these attacks had taken place. Here Dr Francis offered a lifeline. According to his medical opinion, men who had served the army in hot climates could develop a tendency toward epilepsy. Knowing Atherley's medical history, his discharge because of enteric fever (typhoid) and his apparent bouts of depression, lent credence to the idea that his mind could well have been unbalanced at the time he committed the murders. Unfortunately Dr Francis also told the court that throughout his examination of the man in the dock he had seen no evidence of remorse. Atherley it seemed had never once accepted the seriousness of his situation, failed to recognise the awfulness of his actions and had constantly reaffirmed his motive as being one of jealousy. This, as the prosecution were quick to seize upon, destroyed any notion of insanity, as Mr Ryland Adkins said so eloquently:

While no motive was sufficient to justify murder, they knew only too well that of all human passions jealousy was that which most often led to crimes of violence.

The jury agreed, no question of insanity as far as they were concerned and after a short consultation unanimously returned a guilty verdict.

Atherley immediately lodged an appeal. There was still time his counsel argued to prove insanity. Not so according to the courts. The appeal failed and thirty-nine-year-old Samuel Atherley was executed on the morning of 14 December before the prison clock had finished chiming the hour of eight.

Chapter 11

The Great Warsop Mystery 1930

When police constable Holland saw a parked car without lights near to Warsop windmill curiosity got the better of him. After a long day he ought to have cycled past, ignored the lack of lights and just gone home. It was a quarter to one in the morning, the village was quiet, the car would have caused no serious hindrance to anyone that night, but curiosity is a policeman's lot. The car was a Morris-Cowley Tourer, a convertible and the hood was up, perhaps it was this more than the illegal parking that caught the young policeman's eye. Either way as he stepped away from the saddle he could see the car had been driven somewhat erratically before it had come to a halt on the grass verge. The night was damp, tyre tracks could be seen at various places along the edge of the small grass bank on which it rested, where the car had weaved on and off the road before finally coming to rest where he now found it. Cautiously, he shone a flashlight around its body work looking for damage to its panelling or tyres. There was none. But as he moved the light up toward the driver's side of the car he caught a glimpse of a figure, slumped but still behind the wheel of the car. Closer observation showed the figure to be a man, still sat in the driver's seat, head slumped forward, the body leaning more toward the nearside passenger seat. There was blood around his face, chest and left arm and without doubt the occupant was dead. What constable Holland had stumbled upon was a mystery, the kind of which is rare in police circles.

Samuel Fell Wilson, the man PC Holland had found, was a native of Warsop. He was manager of his father's business on Sherwood Street. On Monday nights he always took the car, owned by his father, and used it to drive around the Nottinghamshire villages collecting money owed to the business. That night (23 September) had been no exception. Leaving home at three o'clock in the afternoon he had first

The road where Samuel Wilson's car was found. The author

The windmill at Warsop as it is today. The author

driven over to Clipstone, then on to Ollerton and finally Edwinstowe, which he left at ten minutes to nine that night. All this was clearly recorded in the meticulous written record he maintained, detailing each call he made and the money he had collected. On that particular Monday he had listed his calls and totalled his takings as £21 14s 5d (£21.77p). Of this amount of money he had collected twelve £1 notes, five ten shilling notes and £7 4s 5d (£7.27p) in coin. It was only the coin that remained on the body. For the police motive was obviously simple, Samuel Wilson had been robbed.

When Dr Norman Wilson examined the body at the scene he found two gunshot wounds, one to the left arm and left side of the chest and one to the left side of the face, coupled with two broken ribs also on the left side. At the time his opinion was that the killing had taken place some three to five hours earlier, which put the time of the shooting at between 7.45 pm and 9.45 pm. The post-mortem later on the Tuesday confirmed this initial assessment but did not narrow down the timescale.

Scotland Yard were called in within hours of the investigation being launched and Chief Inspector Barrett and Detective Sergeant Harris arrived during Tuesday morning to take over, famous for capturing Frederick Browne and William Henry Kennedy in 1927. Probably two of the most callous murderers of the early twentieth century after they shot dead police constable George Gutteridge near Howe Green in Essex, shooting him twice in the head and then whilst he lay dying shooting him again in both eyes, the killers being executed in May 1928. So the two policemen came with a reputation that caused a degree of excitement throughout the city and the county's surrounding villages.

Expectations then were very high, both press and local people believing there would be an early resolution to the crime. From the way the case was handled in the first three days these expectations seemed well founded. The two policemen delivering a fresh impetus to the investigation and by midweek offering up the first possible scenario for the murder. Robbery was quite obviously the motive but by midweek the police team had begun to examine the possibility that Samuel Wilson had been shot by a poacher. Possibly a man he knew, perhaps even offered a lift to. Warsop was a rural area; many of its inhabitants owned or were often seen carrying guns. There would have been no reason to suppose anyone he saw that night with a gun cradled in his arm would have stopped him offering a lift provided he knew the man doing the cradling, or so the argument ran. It seemed a logical assertion to make. The wounds they knew by this time had been inflicted by a sporting gun, 12-bore, common for hunting and because of no damage sustained by the car, probably from close range and inside the car with the butt of the gun possibly used to hit Samuel, breaking his ribs.

The intermittent tyre tread patterns along the grass verge first seen by constable Holland ran for some sixty yards. The car had its hand brake on and the lights off when found. All of which indicated that the driver had either been shot before he stopped causing the car to weave along the side of the road, or else there had been a struggle causing the car to constantly veer toward the verge. Either way it seemed clear only the killer could have switched off the lights and quite probably pulled on the hand brake. Fingerprint checks did seem to bear this out, prints being found that did not belong to the driver, giving added credence to the idea being postulated to the press.

Door to door enquiries had revealed that the occupants of two cottages opposite to where the car was found had heard two gunshots at around half past nine on the night of the murder, because gunshots were a common enough occurrence after dark they had not investigated. Yet this frustrating detail, whilst it did little to enhance the killer profile they sought to build up it did

The church at Warsop. The author

Samuel Wilson's grave. The author

enable police to begin narrowing down the time of death. Corroboration of time came from another local, George Parke, who stepped forward to say he saw the car at exactly 9.40 pm, parked where it had been found and without lights. Further enquiries amongst those people Wilson had visited during the evening of his murder, in conjunction with the precise calculation of time versus distance travelled, the route he would have taken and the road on which he was found added to the growing medical evidence that nine thirty was the most likely time for him to have been shot.

At the inquest only one other intriguing piece of evidence found its way into the public domain. When Samuel Wilson had been found, the side window on the driver's side had been open, the window on the nearside closed, meaning nothing of great significance but adding to the growing mystery that had begun to surround his death. The *Nottingham Evening Post* began to speculate that this scene of crime evidence destroyed the theory that had begun to circulate about a gun being thrust through a window of the car to shoot him. He had been shot on his left side, an open window on his right had to discount this notion. They were probably right.

In an article they ran on 2 October they offered up two theories. One, that Wilson had stopped his car, picked up a gun carrying passenger who had fired accidentally after the car had been jolted by the uneven surface of the road. Two, that he had been flagged down by a poacher who had opened the passenger door and then thrust a 12-bore into the car and shot him. Police had already discounted the first notion, one shot could have been accidental, the second could not and of course neither would have broken his ribs. But the second idea had some credence in fact.

The car which Samuel Wilson had driven that night had a running board either side. It was not impossible to speculate that a poacher, known to him, had flagged him down. Once stationary, he had wound down the window on his side of the car, held a brief conversation, offered a lift, which the poacher accepted. He in turn had then walked around to the near side (passenger side) of the car, pulled open the door, pointed the gun at him and demanded money. He would have been familiar with Wilson's collection round habits and aware he was carrying a reasonable amount of cash. Wilson in turn refused, an argument followed. Wilson tried to wrestle the gun away whilst in his seated position. The poacher struck him in the side with the butt of his gun then shot him once. Still alive, Wilson had attempted to drive away but because he had no use in his left arm the car had failed to pick up any speed and had meandered between the road and the grass verge before finally coming to a halt. The poacher meanwhile had chased after him, car door possibly still open, thrust the barrels back into the car's interior and shot its driver a second time, this time in the head. Collecting up the money he could see, possibly kept on the passenger seat, he then calmly walked back around the car to the driver's side, standing on the running board leaned into the car and flicked off the light switch before running off into the night.

It was a theory that seemed to fit the crime scene Constable Holland had found and certainly made a lot of sense to the investigating officers. Yet three hundred statements from villagers and those who lived nearby had resulted in very little. Police contended that the killer was being shielded, possibly by a woman, possibly his wife. A number of appeals were made via the local press but no-one ever stepped forward with information that could have led to any arrest and conviction. As October drew to a close the trail went cold. By Christmas it had been shelved as unsolved and there it has remained.

Chapter 12

A Caring Death –
The Case of Nurse Waddingham
1936

Being placed into the care of nurse Dorothea Nancy Waddingham was to be extremely unfortunate. Dorothy, as she preferred to be called, had no medical qualification to her name. Yet in 1936 she ran a nursing home at 32 Devon Drive, Nottingham for the old, infirm and terminally ill. The fees were reasonable and its appearance professional, sufficient recommendation for those families who chose to send

West Bridgford, c.1900. Nottingham Public Library

their relatives into her dubious care.

Born in Hucknall in 1900, she had embarked upon a life of crime at an early age. In 1925, after working for a short period as maid in the infirmary at Burton on Trent, she came to the attention of police for obtaining two dresses by deception and was bound over for twelve months. Marrying Thomas Leech in 1926 brought about an enforced lull in her burgeoning criminal career whilst she gave birth to two children. This lull lasted for four years during which time her record was clean but then in 1929 she found herself arrested for a second time after attempting to falsely obtain credit of £500. This offence brought with it two years of probation and forced the couple to move into West Bridgford. Here she decided looking after a young family was too arduous a task and placed an advert for a nursery maid for her children. Claiming to be in receipt of £8,000 per year from her father, she interviewed several women before settling on the unlucky Lucy Lebster. Of course there was no substantive income. In fact no rent had been paid on the house for over two years by the time the maid took up her post. Miss Lebster found no wages forthcoming either. In fact she found it was she who, through her employment, had unwittingly been used to subsidise the Leech household. When, after realising she was never to receive a salary, she resigned; it was to discover Dorothy had stolen her gold wristwatch some weeks earlier. The watch had subsequently been pawned and the money raised pocketed. Police were called and Dorothy went to prison for three months.

After her release she and her husband found themselves moving around West Bridgford before agreeing rent on a property in Haydon Road, which they felt they could sub-let. This brought them a reasonable income along with a third child. However, Thomas Leech had been suffering from ill health and after his untimely death in 1932 Dorothy decided to move on. Using the limited knowledge she had gained working out of Burton on Trent infirmary years earlier she obtained a post as District nurse for Carrington. Here she gained considerable expertise in the administration of drugs and at the same time saw a niche in the care market for nursing homes.

Trent Boulevard, West Bridgford, 1907. Nottingham Public Library

Having embarked upon a relationship with a previous tenant, Ronald Sullivan, after the death of her husband it seemed a perfect solution for the two to earn a good income from fee paying patients who needed a place in which to live out their days. That place they decided would be 32 Devon Drive, Nottingham.

On 5 January 1935 Nurse Waddingham, as she had chosen to be called, was paid a visit by Miss Winifred Blagg. This was important, Miss Blagg was a part of the County Nursing Association, the home had been recommended. The reason for her visit was to discuss the plight of two women, a mother and

Devon Drive today. The author

daughter named Baguley, who were both in dire need of care. The mother was eighty-seven years old, her daughter Ada, fifty. It was the daughter who needed the greater care. Unfortunately for Ada, she had been afflicted with a degenerative wasting disease, which was slowly rendering her immobile. She needed round the clock care and all that that entailed, which was quite considerable. Bed-bound for most of her days, she suffered from bed sores which needed daily attention, could not at times feed herself and found it impossible to get in or out of bed without help. But Waddingham was only too willing to take them on. A fee of thirty shillings (£1.50p) each a week was agreed and ten days later mother and daughter left their home at Burton Joyce and moved in. Waddingham believed, after her long discussion with Winifred Blagg that the two women were impoverished. Within a week of their arrival she had discovered her initial assessment had been very wrong.

When Joseph Baguley, Ada's father had died in April 1929 he had left a considerable legacy in trust for his daughter. This consisted of eight cottages in Burton Joyce, worth in the region of £1,600, which were at the time of the two women's arrival at Devon Drive being rented out. Joseph intended that his wife receive the income from the lets until her death though their ownership he had transferred to his daughter. Upon the death of his wife this income resorted to Ada and she was free to dispose of them as she wished.

To Waddingham this meant only one thing, more money. She could see no reason why, with such an estate, each could pay more than the thirty shillings they had all agreed to pay. Toward the end of January she saw her opportunity to broach the subject indirectly. Cousin Laurence Baguley paid a visit to Ada. Waddingham lost no time in taking him aside and telling him in no uncertain terms that the thirty shillings was no longer adequate. Forcefully she told him that the work involved in ensuring Ada had continuing healthcare so that all her needs were met would require a more substantial contribution to the nursing home. Laurence was sympathetic, offering to broker a better deal for her if he could, though it is likely he was merely paying her lip service.

On 27 January that same year Mr Allcock, sub-manager of the

Midland Bank, Netherfield as it is today. The author

Netherfield branch of Midland Bank paid the home a visit. The Baguley's were good clients of the bank, he wanted to ensure their continued good health was being maintained. Waddingham could not resist such a god sent opportunity, here was the man who knew just how much her two patients were actually worth, valuable information indeed. She met him just as he was about to leave. Disappointed by the lack of response to Laurence's visit she felt the credibility of the bank would be a better substitute particularly if that credibility were to back her argument for more money. She told Allcock that she knew the two women were reasonably wealthy, explained her need for increased fees, how she felt she had been misled upon their admittance to the home. Like Laurence before him he was sympathetic but unwilling to help, so Waddingham suggested the two women turned over their estates to her at their death. It would, she argued, be fair recompense if she agreed to care for them both until their deaths. Allcock was less than impressed by the proposal and left.

Eight days later Miss Winifred Blagg who had been responsible for putting her friends into the hands of what she now suspected were unscrupulous carers, wrote a long letter to Laurence Baguley. She had learned of the intention to have the women change their Wills in favour of Waddingham. Aware that Laurence, because of his family ties, had been set the task of executor in Ada's Will she felt it only right he should know of what was about to take place. He in turn wrote a letter to his cousin (Ada) expressing his concerns over the actions she was proposing, outlining in straight forward terms his distrust of the home and in particular Ronald Sullivan.

But plans were moving ahead at an alarming rate. On 9 March 1935 Sullivan paid a visit to Ada Baguley's solicitor, Norman Lane. Unable at that juncture to meet with him but knowing that Lane held the current Will, he agreed to return three weeks later. On 28 March the two men finally sat down to discuss what were ostensibly Ada's wishes. Sullivan outlined what Waddingham had already discussed with the bank, namely that the Wills be redrawn and the key beneficiaries redefined as himself and Dorothea Waddingham. Lane argued strongly against any such proposal, so strongly that Sullivan left his office without setting up the necessary meeting between solicitor and client. It was only a temporary hiccup. A week later, presumably after some discussion about how they should proceed in light of Lane's obstinacy, he was back. After a short meeting, and despite his serious misgivings, Lane agreed with Sullivan's new request that he write to Ada before taking the matter any further. It seemed a perfect solution. Later that same day Laurence Baguley arrived at the home, dissatisfied with all he was hearing and wanting to meet and discuss the idea of new Wills with his cousin. Waddingham refused him admission, telling him he was no longer welcome; Ada had expressed a wish not to ever see him again. True or not he left and moved to Scotland.

One week after Norman Lane's letter had been received Sullivan was back at his office. He told the solicitor that Ada had agreed to the redraft and wanted it actioned. Again, Lane prevaricated, insisting the proposal was fraught with difficulties. But this time Sullivan would not be so easily dissuaded from forcing the solicitors hand. The two men discussed the apparent obstacles, Lane only finally agreeing if all parties were represented by solicitors. A point Sullivan had prepared for; as he left the office he handed over the name of a legal firm who would act on behalf of the home. Reluctantly Lane agreed to meet once all legal parties had been made aware.

Not satisfied with having almost secured new Wills in their favour Waddingham convinced Ada to release money to her from her bank deposit held at Mr Allcocks' bank. There seemed to be little resistance by Ada who happily accompanied Ronald Sullivan to the branch at Netherfield where, after struggling into the bank, she withdrew £50. But the experience had proved difficult to all concerned and not all the money held on account was held in the one passbook Ada possessed at the home. Sullivan wrote a letter, signed by Ada, which he sent on to Norman Lane after she had told him that the solicitor held not only her Will but also her other bank accounts.

So once again he had cause to meet the difficult solicitor

The church at Burton Joyce, near to where Ada Baguley once lived. The author

though there were no issues raised on this occasion. The letter appeared genuine, Sullivan signed to receive the various account books and Lane released them. Over the next few days further withdrawals were made and the account at Netherfield closed. The Will so eagerly sought by Waddingham was finally drawn up and ratified on 4 May, from that point on things began to change.

On 12 May 1935 Ada's mother died. She was an old lady, there was nothing suspicious about her death, and the death certificate was made readily available. At her funeral on the 14th no one expressed the slightest doubt as to the manner of her death the only contentious issue raised was by Waddingham. She found it impossible not to discuss the arrangement Ada had made with her Will and how she and Sullivan were to take care of her for the rest of her days. There were those who felt uncomfortable at the nature of the provision made, but no one challenged the intent.

Perhaps they should have done, on 11 September, without any apparent warning Ada Baguley died. According to Waddingham she had taken a turn for the worse during the evening of 10 September after eating a particularly heavy meal. Both she and Sullivan, she claimed, had stayed up all night with her and in early hours of the following morning she had suffered a stroke, slipped into a coma and died at 10.15 am. The doctor who had treated her throughout her time at Devon Drive, Dr Herbert Mansfield, confirmed death as cerebral haemorrhage and whilst writing up his notes was approached by Sullivan clutching a letter. The letter was for his attention, in Sullivan's own hand, apparently dictated to him by Ada and said that in the event of her death she wished to be cremated. A postscript had been added to the effect that no relatives were to be informed. The doctor took little notice of its content at the time and told Sullivan to take the letter with him to the undertaker where he could complete the necessary forms for cremation.

In accordance with legal requirements Ada was first removed to the mortuary where a post-mortem was to be carried out the following day. Police attended the nursing home routinely and also viewed this letter and the cremation papers. At that stage in proceedings there was little to cause alarm for any of the officials involved. But as 12 September dawned things were to change rapidly.

The routine post-mortem found over 3.192 grains of morphine in the body, more than enough to have caused her death. Police obviously wanted to know where it had come from. Waddingham told them she had administered it orally, in tablet format, the tablets having been given to her by Dr Mansfield on an earlier visit for her to use at her own discretion. According to her it was routine, no more. Police were far from satisfied and when Dr Mansfield denied having ever given morphine for the treatment of Ada Baguley she and Ronald Sullivan were arrested. On 30 September Ada's mother was exhumed and a second post-mortem found morphine in her body too.

The trial, which began on 24 February 1936 before Mr Justice Goddard, attracted huge crowds to Nottingham's Shire Hall. Many eager to obtain the best seats available in the public gallery had been queuing since nine o'clock in the morning on what was a cold, damp day. Others simply wanted to see Waddingham arrive from Birmingham where she had been imprisoned since her arrest. They were to be disappointed; by the time the queue had started forming she was already inside along with Sullivan who had been brought over from Lincoln prison. Once inside those who had been able to gain admission sat in silence as, at a little after ten o'clock, the defendants were brought into court. Waddingham wore a sombre black coat, long scarf and maroon hat. Similarly, Sullivan dressed smartly in a dark suit. Both pleaded not guilty as the charge was read out.

Mr Norman Birkett KC prosecuting for the crown took the floor and addressed the court. In his opening speech he told the jury to expect evidence in support of three main matters appertaining to Ada's murder:

The first was the events which led up to the 11 September – the date of the death of Ada Baguley – and the events which followed closely upon it.

Secondly, what was the interest the prisoners had in desiring the death of Ada Baguley, and what motive they had or could have had in bringing about that death?

Thirdly, what opportunities had they, or either of them of administering the poison?

The trial lasted for most of the week and Mr Birkett managed to prove each point in detail.

As for the chronological order of events leading up to the murder, the first of his points was easily proved, as was the second. It was the third and crucial point that took the greatest amount of difficulty. When Dr Mansfield took the stand everyone knew his testimony was key in identifying just where Waddingham had obtained the morphine. She had insisted since her arrest that it had come from him, that she had done nothing other than treat Ada Baguley with his knowledge and consent. According to her statement, made shortly after her arrest, Dr Mansfield had visited the home on 27 August and had given her six morphia tablets. These were the tablets she had used. But according to his testimony, delivered with damning effect, this was pure fabrication. He had never given morphia to his patient other than as part of a medicine mixed by a chemist, a bottle of Kaolin mixture had been prescribed just before her death, this contained a small amount. As for morphine in tablet form, Ada had no use for it.

Mr Birkett wanted to know where morphine in tablet form could have come from. As the day wore on it became clear. Dr Mansfield had treated a Mrs Kemp and Mrs Harwood both of who had been previous residents of the home run by nurse Waddingham. In the case of Mrs Harwood he had supplied heroin tablets but for Mrs Kemp, unsuited by heroin, he had supplied morphine. These tablets he had handed to the good nurse on a number of visits in quantities of approximately eight at any one time. In just over two months he handed over no fewer than 140 tablets, each half a grain, which he took from a bottle he always carried in his waistcoat pocket. After Mrs Kemp's death he had been given an unused quantity back, which he presumed were all that was left of those he had prescribed. Mr Birkett clearly believed that not to be the case.

On Wednesday morning, 26 February, Mr Justice Goddard directed that Ronald Sullivan be found not guilty of murder. Having listened to two intense days of legal argument and witness evidence, nothing had been heard that could have implied his culpability to murder. He may have been a part of the household, been instrumental in certain aspects of the unsavoury story being slowly unravelled, but there had been no evidence to show he took any part in administering the drug that killed Ada Baguley. For Dorothea Waddingham however, evidence a plenty was arriving in court on a daily basis.

When Dr Roche Lynch, who had carried out the post-mortem, took the stand toward the end of the week it was to confirm that the amount of morphine found in Ada's body could not have been administered gradually. The manner of her death and the quantity found indicated a large dose had been consumed at some point on the night before she died. The court had already heard how Ada had received visitors the evening prior to her death who reported she seemed hale and healthy. If morphine had been administered before their arrival this would not have been the case.

In his summing up Mr Justice Goddard returned to this crucial point and told the jury they had to decide if morphia had been handed over by a doctor or had been hidden away by Waddingham months earlier:

The first great conflict in this case was with regard to the prisoners allegation that on 27 August, Dr Mansfield gave her six tablets which the prisoner assumed to be morphia.

What that means is this, is it not, on 27 August this woman who had been seen by a consulting physician not more than a week before is in such a state that her own doctor is said by the accused to have given this prisoner this drug to be administered at the nurse's discretion.

The doctor says he did not give it to her, and he says, moreover, there was nothing in Ada's condition which would lead him to leave morphia for her.

They obviously felt, having listened to all the evidence, that Waddingham had lied, and after retiring for two hours returned a verdict of guilty, *with a strong recommendation to mercy*. An appeal was instantly launched but finally rejected on 14 April. Two days later Dorothea Nancy Waddingham was executed in Birmingham, though not without incident. By nine o'clock that morning, the time designated by the court, a crowd of several thousand people had begun to build up around the prison precinct. Led by a Mrs Van Der Elst, who arrived driving a white car equipped with loudspeakers, they sang *Abide with Me* surrounded by some two hundred policeman, drafted in to maintain control. It was an unnecessary precaution. The crowd, having made their point, dispersed as easily as it had formed.

Chapter 13

The Walesby Murder
1945

In 1943 Leonard Holmes was serving in the army and stationed in Huddersfield. How long he stayed there is not known but there is no doubting the fact, that despite his wife and six children back home in Walesby, he was far from faithful. At some time during that year he met a young woman, May Shaw, and began a relationship. For Holmes this relationship was both serious and necessary. Whether or not his marriage was unhappy is unclear but certainly he intended to end it at some stage and if possible move his children north. May had apparently agreed to this idea, expecting Holmes to force the issue once home and make the necessary break. But there was a war on, Holmes was a serving soldier, breaking up a marriage under those circumstances was not to be easy.

Nothing happened during 1944, in fact it was not until November the following year that things came to a head. On Saturday, 17 November Leonard Holmes parents paid the family a visit. At some point that evening they, along with Leonard and his wife Peggy, all walked down to the *Carpenters Arms* public house. Everything appeared to be normal, he and has wife gave the impression they were happily married; certainly there was no outward indication that their relationship was under any pressure. Inside Holmes was probably quietly seething.

After returning home and after his parents departure a row developed between husband and wife. It amounted to very little and the two of them went to bed. For Holmes, however, the argument was unresolved. Whilst they had all been in the pub that night he claimed to have seen his wife giving *certain nods and a wink* to two RAF airmen who had been stood at the bar. At some point late on the following day, Sunday, he brought up the point again and began to accuse her of being unfaithful. She ridiculed the idea whilst at the same time countered his

Carpenters Arms, *Walesby.* Nottingham Public Library

accusation with her knowledge of his association with May Shaw. There seems little doubt she knew some of what had taken place in Huddersfield though there was no evidence to suggest she ever suspected infidelity. Whatever, the very fact she had dared raise the subject, claimed Holmes later, enraged him beyond anything she could possibly have intended. Reaching for the coal hammer he struck her once to the side of the head. The blow was sufficient to knock her down but not kill her. As she lay prostrate on the floor, unable to raise herself up, no doubt suddenly aware of what was about to happen, Holmes climbed on top of her, placed his hands around her neck and strangled her to death. According to the time given at his trial it was 2.04 am.

Walesby today. The author

Children in the house meant that he needed to work through the night if he was to ensure their continued ignorance of the killing. Carefully he washed his bloodstained clothes, cleaned away any stains from the floor and saw to their breakfast on the Monday morning. After delivering them all safely to school he told them to go to their grandparents that night then set out for Huddersfield and May Shaw telling her on his arrival that Peggy had left him and would not be returning.

Unfortunately for Holmes, whilst he was in Huddersfield his brother had paid an unexpected visit to his home in Walseby and discovered Peggy's body. When he travelled back on the Tuesday evening police were waiting for him and arrested him at Retford. He was charged at 4 am on Wednesday morning with the murder and made no denial:

> *Yes, it happened on Sunday night. It was over something she said. I hit her with a hammer head...There is only one answer to the charge. I admit it.*

At his trial before Mr Justice Charles on 28 February he pleaded not guilty. It was to prove a futile attempt at trying to argue that the killing was manslaughter, that he had killed as a result of an argument, not that he had ever intended murder. He may well have won his case had it not been for a telegram. A telegram, which when the court sat on the 28th could not at first be produced but when found proved very damning.

Leonard Holmes had sent a telegram dated 17 November, which was the Saturday all the family had gone out for a drink to the *Carpenters Arms*. It had been sent to May Shaw in Huddersfield preparing the ground for his visit on the coming Monday: 'See you Sunday or Monday for sure. Be prepared. OK. All fixed. Len'

If, as he had claimed since his arrest, the killing was not premeditated but a violent reaction during a fierce argument, why send it? The suggestion to its recipient was obvious. Things had been sorted out, and he was splitting from Peggy, however that was to be achieved. It also implied that Holmes had devised a plan to rid himself of his wife and that that plan had been

New Ollerton. The author

pieced together before everyone went out on Saturday night. When he had picked up the hammer he had done so with the intention of committing a planned murder, in other words the killing was premeditated. Holmes of course refuted this version of events claiming instead that he had seen a packed suitcase. This he insisted was what had prompted the telegram, the suitcase belonged to his wife and the significance of its discovery was that he knew she intended to leave him. He simply wanted May Shaw prepared for his arrival on the Monday.

Professor Webster, Director of West Midland Forensic Laboratory, gave further credence to the murder theory when he told the court that in his opinion Peggy Holmes would probably have survived the initial hammer blow. It was the strangulation that caused her death, which lent weight to the prosecution argument that, had it been simply a domestic row, he would have stopped after striking her. The fact that he did not and had also sent a telegram to Huddersfield before the attack were key indicators as to his intent.

The jury agreed and brought in a guilty verdict. A subsequent appeal to the House of Lords failed and he was executed at Lincoln prison on 28 May 1946.

Chapter 14

The Death of the Borstal Matron
1948

When Kenneth Strickson became an inmate of Sherwood Borstal Institution in June 1947 he was merely continuing a path he had begun years earlier. Already having served a period in an Approved school, he found himself, at twenty-one years of age, spiralling inexorably down a well worn criminal highway, along which potential and promise were abandoned in favour of corruption and delinquency. Though whether or not he saw it quite that way is debateable. If he did he certainly had not heeded the warning signs.

As part of his duties within the institute he to was clean out the chapel wing when required and assist the matron, who had control over the area, whenever she was working in the vestry. For Strickson, starved of female contact, it was manna from heaven. Forty-six-year-old Irene Phillips had been matron for only one year. She was one of two matrons operating in the institution and the one he found more attractive. Unfortunately for her, he also believed she was attracted to him, that his thoughts and feelings were reciprocated.

Each morning at around half-past-seven the inmates were allowed to gather in the recreation room. It was a social session, a little interaction where the inmates could chat amongst themselves, observed but generally free of the normal daily restrictions that governed their lives. Here, on 18 November, five months after his admission, Strickson let it be known during a conversation with fellow inmate Enoch Roberts, possibly for the first time, that his interest in Irene Phillips was about to go beyond that which he knew to be appropriate. On the previous day he had made reference to her figure, a sexual comment, something intended to elicit a response. He probably expected some sort of censure or reproof, but Irene Phillips had worked

Bagthorpe Gaol today.. The author

in the area of youth custody for many years before accepting the post of matron at Nottingham. Working around young men she had learned to accept sexual innuendo without feeling threatened. She thought it best to take the comment, as she believed Strickson had intended it, in no more than jest and so treated it as such, telling him she was broad minded. It was a mistake. Strickson had probably expected an instant rebuke and when she failed to react negatively he saw it as form of enticement.

Twenty-four hours after this conversation had taken place the two men once again joined up at the start of the day and once again Strickson's thoughts turned to Irene Phillips. He told Roberts what he intended to do that morning:

> *I am going up to the chapel with matron and I am going to have a go at her up there. I am going to see what I can get out of her.*

Roberts read into that a deal of intent and told Strickson that what he was suggesting would get him three years in prison. But Strickson was not to be dissuaded. The two men discussed it further. In Roberts's later testimony he stated that Strickson obviously believed there would be no serious repercussions to any sexual advances he made, his view seemed to be that she would only perhaps fight against him. Roberts asked what he would do if she screamed: 'I should cosh her in the head if she did.'

So, resolute about what he intended to do that morning, he left the recreation room as the various groups split and headed off to the chapel. But Irene had been delayed. A fruitless search of the various rooms and area's that she controlled had failed to locate her and it was not until after ten thirty that he managed to track her down. What happened next has never been fully explained, but at some point the two obviously did meet and that meeting took place in the vestry.

At around 11 am Harry Bradshaw, a former inmate was also looking for the matron. He came to the vestry because he knew it was the most obvious place to find her. When no one answered his knock he tried the door, which he found to be locked. Had it not been for the fact that he believed he could hear someone breathing he would have walked away, as it was curiosity got the better of him. Crouching down he put his eye to the keyhole whilst propping himself up with a hand on the floor. Suddenly he became aware that the floor appeared to be wet, taking his eye from the door he looked down and saw a growing pool of blood seeping out into the corridor.

Whilst this was taking place Strickson was standing outside trying to obtain permission to join a building party that was leaving by the front gate. Turned away without a pass he was sent to find Christopher Morrow who had the necessary authority to release him from the institute's confines. During the time it took him to walk from the gate to wherever Christopher

Governor's house, Bagthorpe Gaol. The author

Morrow had his desk, which could not have been long, he had a change of heart. Instead of requesting a pass he simply asked if the man would go to the chapel because he had killed the matron.

Irene Phillips lay where he had left her, on the floor of the vestry, her body twisted in a grotesque fashion but still alive. When Morrow unlocked the vestry door he could clearly see she had sustained severe head injuries, the blood from which had so scared Harry Bradshaw. Scattered around her were the broken remains of two wooden chairs, parts of which had been used to inflict the injuries. She was taken to hospital but died within forty-five minutes of being admitted. Strickson was obviously arrested but had no explanation for why he had carried out the attack. According to Detective Inspector Reginald Corbett who interviewed him, Strickson appeared to be frightened, speaking only in a whisper and when told he was to be arrested for the attack all he said was: 'Yes, I don't know why I did it.'

In evidence at his trial before Mr Justice Lynskey on 2 March 1949, professor J M Webster, Director of the Home Office Laboratory at Birmingham, told the court that Irene Phillips had sustained injuries of three types. There were bruises to the arms, chest, and abdomen, abrasions to the left side of her face, lacerations to the back of her head and fractures to her skull and spine. The attack had been frenzied and much of it whilst she was on the ground, but the attack had not been sexual. Strickson refused to say just what had taken place inside that vestry, his counsel pleading insanity at the time of the killing. Arguing strongly that the condition ran in his family, his grandfather having supposedly died in a mental institution.

The jury were having none of it and returned a verdict of guilty after only twenty-two minutes spent in deliberation. An appeal was immediately launched claiming that an electroencephalograph, which registers the electrical activity of the brain, showed signs of anomalous brain activity. Coupled with an epileptic condition believed to have been suffered by his father, which in turn had been blamed for a decline in the man's mental capability, meant that Strickson must have been insane at the time he committed the murder. The report had already been aired in full during the trial but because it was a medical diagnosis of a highly technical nature its content had possibly not been given the proper hearing it deserved. Leastways that was the defence argument for using it a second time. It made little difference. The Home Secretary rejected it on 21 March just as Mr Justice Lynskey had done, stating that there were insufficient grounds for granting a reprieve. There was nothing left in Strickson's defence that could have explained his moment of madness and he paid the ultimate price in Lincoln Prison on the following day.

Chapter 15

The Suspicious Death of Florence Weatherall 1951

When Henry Harrison stepped out of his caravan on the evening of 23 February 1951 he solved a three-week-old puzzle and began a mystery that still exists today. Positioned as it was, the caravan stood on Moor Road, Bestwood, a lonely stretch of roadway beside Goosedale farm. Whenever he needed water he had to fetch it from a spring that ran just beyond the farm gate. On this particular night as he passed through the gateway he saw what he at first thought to be a tailor's dummy or a manikin. It lay face down in the ditch that ran beside the hedgerow. Curious, he decided having drawn his water to take a closer look. What he had found as he peered

Linby village. The author

Linby Church. The author

down into the murky depths was the body of a woman. She lay in water on her side; a brown tailored overcoat covered the upper part of the body, pulled down at each shoulder, beneath that was a blue woollen jumper. She was naked from the waist down except for a pair of nylon stockings and scattered in the ditch around her were a skirt and various under garments. He had found Florence Weatherall.

For three weeks the *Nottingham Evening Post* had reported her disappearance and police had been scouring the countryside in an attempt to find out what had happened to the Linby woman. She had disappeared after leaving the bungalow she and her husband

Ted (Edward) shared on the edge of Ravenswood opposite the main gates to Newstead Abbey. Five days earlier she had given birth to twin girls, Ann and Elizabeth, only leaving hospital on 28 January. According to her mother, Violet Divito, her daughter had left the house in order to register the birth of the two girls and to do a little shopping. She had arrived at the bungalow to do a little baby sitting whilst all this was done and to allow Ted to return to work after having two days off to help his wife after her return from hospital. Florence had left home at twenty minutes to four and had stood opposite the bungalow waiting for a bus; the two women had waved to each other on two or three occasions as Violet caught glimpses of her through the window. Unfortunately for the police, her mother had not seen her actually catch a bus. So the enquiry had developed around the possibility that she had accepted a lift. It was a known fact that she did from time to time accept lifts from passing cars; the road was lonely and buses infrequent.

When her body was found in the ditch beside what is today Bestwood Road, the idea of some stranger in a car picking her up was confirmed. Professor Webster, Director of the West Midlands Forensic Science Laboratory at Birmingham, who carried out the post mortem, was of the opinion that she had been in the ditch since the day of her disappearance. The findings of his examination were that she had died from asphyxia, but that there were a number of strange factors attached to her death. She showed no signs of serious sexual assault though sex had taken place shortly before death, only light bruising on both sides of the neck indicated force, this bruising caused by the right thumb; rigor mortis had set in after she had been placed in the ditch and the hyoid bone, a small easily broken bone found in the larynx was intact. So had police found a murder victim, a suicide or an accident? Suicide was quickly ruled out but the other two possibilities could not be discounted.

Scotland Yard were called in hours after the body's discovery, Superintendent Reginald Spooner and Detective Sergeant Carter arriving in Nottingham on Saturday, 24 February. Spooner came with a reputation. Attached to MI5 during the Second World War he had been one of the arresting officers of

Bestwood Road, near to where the body was found. The author

Lord Haw-Haw, the British born broadcaster who had used radio to broadcast Hitler's propaganda from Germany to the UK, a much detested man whose actions were considered traitorous by a public who had listened each evening to his reports of British losses in the various theatres of war. Spooner had also handled a number of high profile murder cases over the past four or five years and was highly regarded by most who had worked with him.

From the outset Superintendent Spooner was unconvinced as to the motive behind the killing, though he maintained an investigative team whose premise remained murder. He, like Professor Webster, struggled with some of the evidence and in particular the skirt Florence had worn when she set out from home on 2 February. After close examination of all the clothing

Det. Supt. Spooner examining the crime scene. Nottingham Evening Post

Photographing the scene. Nottingham Evening Post

found around her body only the skirt had revealed anything of note. Inside a pocket had been found a large safety pin, but only one, and it was this fact that he found so intriguing. It had no reason to be there, it appeared to serve no purpose yet he felt it to be integral to the investigation he had set in motion. He also wanted to find the handbag, not found at the crime scene and her shopping bag, described as wicker with woven, coloured flowers along its edge. Police by this time had already established that Florence might well, at some stage late on the afternoon she disappeared, have been in Mansfield. Two sightings had been reported before the discovery of her body and both by people who knew her as a woman who had sometimes bought goods from market stalls they owned. Having recently been in hospital giving birth to her daughters, police were confident these witness sightings were accurate simply because she had been out of circulation for a few weeks, they would remember more readily a woman not seen for some time as opposed to a woman seen on a regular basis. If they could find the shopping basket perhaps they could prove some of her movements. The only certainty they felt they had, was that whether or not she had shopped that afternoon, someone had certainly given her a lift. To be found on the Nottingham road at Bestwood some four miles south of her home gave credence to the fact that she had shared a car. It was too remote a location to mean anything else. They began to investigate the people she knew.

Nottinghamshire police, headed by Detective Superintendent Shand, set four questions to be answered by the investigating team:

> *Did Mrs Weatherall really catch a bus?*
> *Did she go to Mansfield?*
> *Did she meet an old friend unexpectedly?*
> *Did she accept a lift from a stranger and never get out of the car alive?*

By the end of February the team had been unable to prove any of them. Certainly there was evidence in support of a visit to Mansfield but not certain. During questioning the two key witnesses to a sighting struggled to confirm the date and bus drivers on the route had not been able to confirm picking up a passenger from the stop outside the Weatherall house. This in turn led to the growing belief that perhaps the stall holders had been mistaken, confused the dates or else someone had possibly stopped to offer a lift and stayed with her, or even arranged a meeting after her shopping trip to take her home. No friend could be found who had seen her on the day she disappeared so it was the latter argument that began to gain credence.

Superintendent Spooner began to postulate the idea that a man, probably someone she knew, had collected her in a car, taken her to Mansfield then headed back to Nottingham and

The ditch where Florence Weatherall was discovered. The author

stopped in the remote area of Goosedale farm, which lies
about three miles south of Linby. The reason for the stop had
been sex, there was evidence sex had taken place before the
killing, therefore, it seemed a perfectly rational explanation
that the car was stopped for that purpose. Nothing found or

produced seemed to support the idea that she had been raped, it appeared to have been consensual. The breakthrough came on 30 May when the missing handbag was found on the main Hucknall to Nottingham road at Bulwell Forest golf club.

Two men searching for lost golf balls found it in a hole over which grass had grown. The men were prodding golf clubs into holes left by fence posts after the boundary fence had been moved back some months earlier. In one such hole, covered over by sods of grass which appeared to have been deliberately placed to hide its location, they discovered the bag. It had clearly been there for some weeks because of its state and had apparently remained unopened. Inside police found a purse, a ration book, several letters and a large safety pin. It was this last item that interested Superintendent Spooner more than any other. For him it solved a key question. Did Florence Weatherall accept a lift in a car and did she know the driver? The answer was an emphatic yes!

Superintendent Spooner believed the discovery of this second safety pin told its own story. Mrs Weatherall had been heavily pregnant running up to Christmas and throughout January. This meant she had not been able to fit into her normal clothes. Since the birth of her twins her size and shape had obviously changed but still not sufficiently for her to fit into skirts she would have been able to wear nine or ten months earlier, hence the safety pins. Discovering two meant that she used them to hold her skirt up when she could not fasten the zipper. If one was found in her coat pocket and one in her handbag then she had removed her lower clothing voluntarily, taking time over removing her skirt and putting the safety pins where they could be easily retrieved. If that was the case, so his argument ran, it was highly likely she knew the man who had almost certainly offered her a lift. But had she been murdered or had her death, though suspicious, been no more than a tragic accident?

By this time police had begun to receive information suggesting that the trip out on 2 February was not her first. Witnesses had come forward claiming to have seen her earlier that same week. It had also been confirmed that she had not

The handbag found stuffed into a post hole. Nottingham Evening Post

registered the children's birth because she had not taken the necessary documentation with her when she had left the house. Her sister, seventeen-year-old Rhona Divito had also provided police with a list of friends or contacts that she knew her sister to have made and possibly maintained. According to the *Nottingham Evening Post* this list comprised of some fourteen men including several fairground people, which prompted enquiries throughout the north of England and a number of travellers or salesmen. So inevitably the enquiry began to swing toward the belief that Florence had possibly arranged a meeting whether with an old friend or some other acquaintance. Spooner was satisfied she had been inside a car and that her death had taken place whilst a passenger. The how and the why he was still attempting to clarify.

When the inquest opened on Wednesday 6 June at Hucknall he was reasonably sure he had the answer. After hearing evidence from her husband, who cleared up the mystery of whether or not she had been out of the house for any period prior to her disappearance, stating she went out the day after her discharge from hospital ostensibly to visit her sister. The court heard how Florence often accepted lifts and how on the day of her disappearance she had stood on the opposite side of the road to the bus stop. Violet Divito, who had waved to her from the house, had a clear view of her for several minutes:

I saw her walking up and down on the side of Mansfield road and we waved to each other three times. She would have to cross the road to catch a bus.

Two buses passed the spot where Florence stood at four o'clock that afternoon; unfortunately no one ever saw her board one of them.

When Professor Webster of the Forensic Science laboratories took the stand he told coroner, Mr A C Mack, that apart from being fully clothed above the waist she wore a coloured scarf around her neck. This though had not caused the bruising he had found. The coroner wanted to know if, as rumour would have it, she had been killed elsewhere and then taken to the ditch in which she was found.

Coroner: Do you feel in all probability she was not murdered in the ditch but in a car and dumped there?

Professor Webster: There is no question that the body was dead when it was put into the water...I think she was not murdered in the ditch but probably in a car and dumped there before rigor mortis set in and the clothing thrown in afterwards.

Professor Webster went on to agree with the Superintendent's theory that her clothing had been removed voluntarily. Furthermore, he was of the belief that the overcoat, which was found pulled down around her shoulders, had not been used to pinion her arms but had merely slipped as her body was being carried from this car to the water filled ditch. The bruising, he explained, had caused her death by producing pressure to her neck, which in turn had stopped the flow of blood to her head. However, this same pressure was not caused by a mere grab but possibly subconsciously by the right thumb of another person.

What the court wanted to know was whether or not Florence Weatherall could have met her death at the hands of a man who had not realised that whilst the two of them were having sex he was killing her. It seemed a plausible argument. Superintendent Shand, who had worked alongside the Scotland Yard detectives, told the jury of nine men that there was sufficient evidence to show she had been involved with other men over the past few years.

Coroner: Prior to her marriage she was a most promiscuous young lady?

Supt. Shand : Yes.

He went on to explain that during the investigation he had found a man, not named, who had met with Florence throughout 1948 three or four times each week, the relationship lasting for twelve months. She had continued through 1949 with a market trader whom she met every Friday and there were others at that time. But it was not so much the relationships that mattered for the coroner's jury but what these men had said about her abnormal or sometimes violent sexual reactions.

In Iain Adamson's book, *The Great Detective,* published in 1966, Superintendent Spooner offered the explanation that because the hyoid bone had not been fractured and in murder by strangulation it always was, then the death had to have been accidental. In the testimony he gave to the court, not recorded by the local press, this was his considered opinion. Certainly the coroner in his summing up told the all male jury they had to decide if they agreed or whether her death was murder, manslaughter or found dead. They took only ten minutes to return the latter. The death was undoubtedly suspicious and someone had almost certainly caused it but in deciding upon an open verdict the case finally came to a close.

Chapter 16

The Price of Fame –
The Murder of Mabel Tattershaw
1951

ineteen-year-old Herbert Leonard Mills was a gambler. Known for his success on the turf, where he played with large stakes, he decided in August 1951 to increase those stakes and make the ultimate gamble, with his life. It is doubtful if he ever considered the price too high. He

Herbert Leonard Mills. Nottingham Evening Post

knew the risks he would have to take, though it is doubtful he ever truly considered what would happen if he lost. Mabel Tattershaw, on the other hand, was just the opposite. She knew nothing of gambling, had no money, no job and worse of all, no luck. What she did not realise when she left her house on 2 August that year was that it was her life he would be gambling with.

Since her husband's conviction and subsequent prison sentence, Mabel had been living a solitary existence. Dependent upon friends for gifts of money or food to help her get by, it was fair to say she found each day a struggle. Her escape from life's drudgery was the cinema. She was an avid fan of the make believe world conjured up by Hollywood, visiting different cinemas on different days of the week. Never alone on these outings, she would share the experience with a woman friend, Lily Wilson, who also enjoyed the big screen world. On 2 August 1951 the two women went to the Roxy Cinema at around half past five in the evening. During the interval Lily noticed Mabel, deep in conversation with a man who had taken the seat beside her. What they discussed she could not hear but she did later recognise the man as Leonard Mills. On the following day at around 5 pm Lillian Oldhouse, who lodged with Mabel, saw her leave the house. She had no idea where she was going but presumed it would be another cinema outing in the city. It was the last time she would ever see Mabel alive. On Saturday morning, 4 August, she reported Mabel missing.

On Wednesday, 8 August Norman Rae, chief crime reporter for the *News of the World* took a telephone call from a man who claimed to have details of a Nottingham murder. He offered to give Rae an exclusive story and photographs of the body if Rae would pay him £250. According to testimony Rae gave later in court the caller told him, that in his opinion, the woman had been strangled and her body dumped. The man gave his name as Leonard Mills. Well aware of what the implications were of becoming embroiled in a murder case without police involvement Rae told Mills that he would call him back later that same evening and Mills provided a call box telephone number for him to use. As Mills waited for the phone to ring Rae of course informed Nottingham police, they in turn arrived

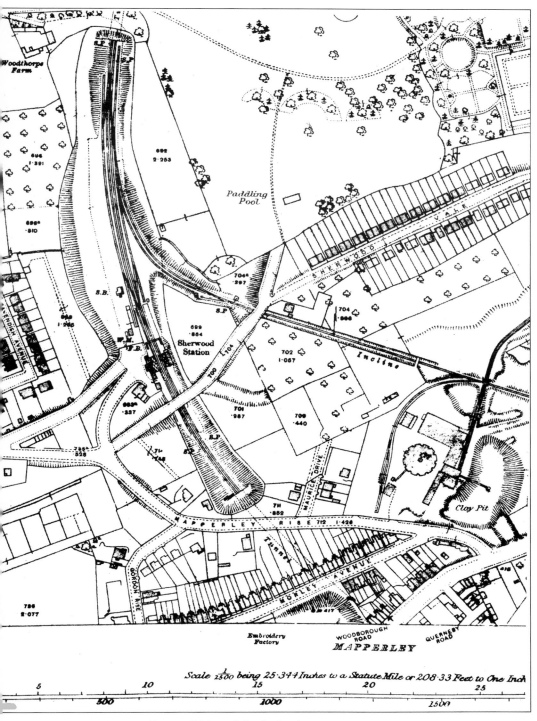

1938 map showing Sherwood Vale and the Orchard. Nottingham Public Library

Sherwood Vale today.

at the phone box just as Mills began his second conversation. Unfazed by their unexpected arrival Mills simply hung up then told them of the body he had found, producing a bead necklace, which he claimed he had found close to where the woman lay.

Later that same day Mills took Detective Sergeant Burrows to Sherwood Vale. Beyond the road lay a small copse known as Hickling's Orchard, locally called the jungle because of its overgrown state. Mills took the policeman through thick brambles and high weeds until he came to a small ravine at the bottom of which could be seen the body of a woman. He indicated the spot where he had found the necklace, which was at the top of this ravine and pointed out that from its location the body could be clearly seen. He made a statement later to that effect claiming to have stumbled across the murder scene during that same day.

On 11 August, Norman Rae took him to London. En route Mills saw a number of newspaper headlines trumpeting the discovery of a body being found in Nottingham, which had suffered a serious battering, sustaining head injuries as a result. Mills became agitated, telling Rae that the woman had sustained nothing of the sort, that her face was pure white and that she had been strangled. Scornful of the news reportage, he insisted there was no reason to claim such outrageous things when he knew them to be untrue. He was paid £75 for the information he provided.

On the following day he tried hard to whip up competition amongst the Daily's, doing all he could to raise the price for his story and making it obvious he would only sell to the highest bidder. But here he made his first notable error; he contradicted himself over the date he claimed to have found the body, identified by this time as Mabel Tattershaw. Instead of Wednesday, the day he had had the telephone conversation with Norman Rae he told *Daily Express* reporter Donald Seaman it had been Sunday, three days earlier. For Mills this was bad news, it meant he had known of a murder for at least four days by the time police were informed. Having once let the fact slip he could not easily retract so he claimed an error, a mistake in remembering the day and tried to let it pass. It would come back to haunt him.

There were further errors to come. In a three-hour interview with Edward Connolly of the *Daily Graphic* he said he had spent some ten minutes with the body in Hickling's orchard. He described seeing her face and it having a streak of blood across the upper lip, he likened the effect to that of a toothbrush moustache. He also elaborated on why he had kept the necklace. It had his fingerprints all over it; once he had handled it he decided it would be better to keep it. The conversation with Connolly though centred mainly around money. Mills, it seems, was obsessed with the opportunity of making capital out of murder to the point that at one stage he said quite openly that he knew newspapers would pay high prices for the life stories of those acquitted of murder. It appeared Herbert Mills was enjoying his moment of fame.

The police on the other hand were struggling to find any motive for the murder. Despite having one key suspect in Mills, there was, at this stage, no serious evidence to link him to the killing. They had verified Mabel Tattershaw's movements up to a point, but still did not know who she had met on the night of her death, or why. That was about to change. Dissatisfied with the progress being made Mills arranged another meeting with Norman Rae. The two met in a Nottingham hotel and in the early of the morning on 23 August Mills took a slip of the hotel's headed notepaper and set out a statement that would eventually hang him:

I, Herbert Leonard Mills state that on the evening of August 8 I killed Mrs Tattershaw and now wish to clear my conscience and confess the murder.

(here followed Mills' signature)

Dated this 25th August. I Herbert Leonard Mills of my own free will without any pressure or force of any kind whatsoever wish to confess to the murder of Mrs Tattershaw. On the evening of August 7, Thursday, I was sitting in the Roxy cinema, two women entered, sitting beside me in the same row.

One woman endeavoured to make conversation. Not wishing to be impolite I answered trying to make it clear I did not wish it. She persisted. At one period she was a little suggestive. She invited me to see her the following day. I refused. She persisted.

I had always considered the possibility of the perfect crime – murder. Here was my opportunity. I have been most successful, no motive, no clues. Why, if I had not reported finding the body I should not have been connected in any manner whatsoever. I am quite proud of my achievement.

Seeing the possibility of putting my theory into practice I consented to meeting her on the morrow. I met her the following day, Friday, August 3. I met her on Edwards Lane. She had told me she would come by that route. We walked down a side turning which approached the Metropole, where we had arranged to meet.

We entered the orchard walking up a path... she took off her coat and lay down. I asked her if I could have the beads she wore... She broke the beads from her neck to give to me... I was satisfied I had found the perfect victim. She said she was cold. I covered her with her own coat, then my own coat...

The strangling itself was quite easily accomplished...I slid her down the bank, covered the coat over her, then left...

Rae told him after reading it through that he would have to hand it to the police. Mills seemed not in the slightest bit concerned and so on the following morning Rae met with Superintendent Ellington and handed over the confession. Mills had played his final card, for him the game was now on. The test for the police was to prove the confession was true and accurate, that it did tell the story of Mabel's death, offered up a motive and that Mills was indeed the real killer. He was duly arrested.

For the next four months a painstaking investigation was carried out. Lily Wilson came forward to tell of the fateful trip she had made to the cinema when Mills had sat beside Mabel. Two other witnesses were found who told of seeing Mills with a woman they believed to have been Mabel on the night she died and most telling of all, forensic examination of both the victim and the supposed killer yielded some pretty damning results. Three hairs were found on Mabel's body which closely matched Mills. Blood was found on his coat which matched Mabel's and skin under her finger nails was, they argued, most likely that of Mills. He meantime seemed unconcerned by his plight. In a letter to a friend, Miss June Brown, dated 21 September he said he was undecided about whether or not he would plead guilty or not guilty, adding a little poetry to emphasis his point:

> *Though so many would believe*
> *This tale is most untrue*
> *Who sells the news on Saturday*
> *On Friday that he slew.*

When his trial opened before Mr Justice Byrne on 19 November he was of the belief that he would be acquitted, that the trial was merely a formality and once evidence as to the inaccuracy of his statement to Norman Rae was heard he would walk free. He had by this time made a second statement, this time to the police. In this he confirmed he had met Mabel but that instead of murdering her he had left her on the corner of Mansfield Road. According to this revised version of events when he met up with Mabel in the cold light of day he found her to be rather shabby, not

*The stairway leading to
Court No. 1, Shire Hall.*
The author

someone he would have wanted people to see him with. They walked for only about ten minutes he claimed. During this time she told him of her husband in jail, of how her daughter had been left pregnant by the lodger who had also gone to prison and how her life had not been easy over the past few years. But he was unimpressed, in his testimony to the court he was adamant that he had told her that he did not want to stay in her company, that meeting was a mistake and had left her, caught a bus into the city and gone to the Scala cinema.

Perfectly plausible except that in his original confession and other conversations with newspaper reporters he had stated facts about the body he purported to have found which suggested this was simply a pack of lies. According to Home Office Pathologist, Mr Webster, Mabel had been battered about the head before being strangled. Anyone discovering her days later would have clearly seen that, strangulation was far from obvious and unproven until the post-mortem had been carried out. The blood Mills had described, as a *toothbrush moustache* would probably have been evident in that guise only immediately after her killing. Once the body had been left she bled from the nose, which covered her entire face. The prosecution argued forcefully that when Mills made his various statements to Norman Rae he was remembering Mabel the only way he could, minutes after having killed her. Only at that point, so the argument ran, would Mabel Tattershaw have appeared almost unblemished.

Nevertheless, throughout his two hours or so on the stand in Nottingham's Shire Hall, Mills stubbornly refused to admit his guilt, though he did have to acknowledge the fact that he was very familiar with the murder site. Apparently Mills, a fan of poetry, often walked through the Orchard area or sat reading *Shelley* on warm days. He also admitted that the reason behind his being in the wood on the day he found the body was because he had intended to sit and read. So his reason to be there was not quite as he had intended people to believe. The orchard rather than being a place he seldom visited, which made his discovery of Mabel appear to be coincidental with a rare visit, was nothing of the sort. Furthermore, intentional or not he was extremely forthcoming as to his intent with the press. He had obviously

The entrance to the Orchard today.

decided to attempt to sell what he saw as a sensational story to the *News of the World*, aware that the price for what he had to say would be substantially increased if he were to be acquitted. Profit, that according to prosecution counsel, was the sole reason for murder. Not so according to Mills. Profit was behind the hotel confession, no more. Mills contended that the document he had drawn and signed was designed to make him money. He wanted to help the police in their search for the real killer and believed strongly that any court would discredit the same document. At the same time its notoriety would bring him momentary fame followed by considerable wealth as he sold his story of wrongful arrest and trial to what he hoped would be a grasping press. Unfortunately for him it had brought about the opposite effect.

Dr Prewer, medical officer of Lincoln prison, attested to this apparent confidence shown by his prisoner. There was, he stated, a 'curious unconcern', and a genuine delight in the amount of publicity his arrest had generated. Whether this was simply a misguided belief that he would be released at some point or that he suffered from some form of self delusion was not discussed. Certainly his defence, ably mounted by Mr R E A Elwes believed so. They seized upon Dr Prewer who went on to say that he saw Mills as an exhibitionist who wanted to be in the limelight, but not a sadist, not a man of violence.

In his speech to the jury Mr Elwes used this testimony to

assert his belief that Herbert Mills had made a statement intended for the press, which was full of 'childish vanity obviously fed on cheap fiction', nothing more than fictional nonsense full of inconsistencies. He sited the notion that Mills had slid Mabel's body down the steep bank or ravine, something he claimed to have done in his confession. Photographs taken at scene of crime, contended Elwes, had failed to show any such possibility. The ground, covered in fallen leaves, showed no sign of being disturbed. He expressed an opinion that the murder, because of this single fact, could not have been carried out at the spot upon which she was found. It must have been done elsewhere and with far more violence than even Mills had supposed. Powerfully, he contested the prosecution case that Mills had intended murder the night he met Mabel Tattershaw. Emphasising Mills, non violent tendencies as testified by the prison doctor had to preclude him from any kind of murderous intent. Then, taking up a sheet of paper, he read one stanza of a poem written by the accused man:

> *From your eyes there is no succour*
> *I am quite helpless in your power*
> *Dearest fairest is this your hour?*
> *Do not my heart deny*
> *For by the power of your eye*
> *I am doomed to live or die*
> *All is yours I have to give*
> *You are all for which I care to live*
> *To thee I pledge to constant be*
> *I love thee to eternity*

It was powerful stuff. But it did not impress the jury. After listening to Mr Justice Byrne's summing up, in which he told them a verdict of insane would be unacceptable, they had to decide how much Mills had gambled and whether or not Mabel Tattershaw was an almost random killing. A killing meant to satisfy a craving and to create an opportunity to sell a story. They believed that to be the case and after twenty-six minutes brought back a guilty verdict. Herbert Leonard Mills was finally executed at Lincoln prison on 11 December 1951. He was still only nineteen years old.

Index